IMAGES
of Sport

NEATH RFC
1871-1945

29

Bill Jones – a legendary Neath figure who captained the Welsh All Blacks for a record number of seasons.

IMAGES
of Sport

NEATH RFC
1871-1945

Mike Price

TEMPUS

1898/99 Neath line-up. Played 34, Won 21, Drawn 5, Lost 8, Points For 273, Points Against 78.

First published 2002, reprinted 2003

Tempus Publishing Limited
The Mill, Brimscombe Port,
Stroud, Gloucestershire, GL5 2QG

British Library Cataloguing in Publication Data.
A catalogue record for this book is available from the British Library.

ISBN 0 7524 2709 0

Typesetting and origination by Tempus Publishing Limited
Printed in Great Britain by Midway Colour Print, Wiltshire

Contents

Introduction

The first-ever newspaper report of a rugby football match played in Wales appeared in the now-defunct *Swansea & Glamorgan Herald* in February 1872. The two teams involved, Neath and Swansea, played out the game to a result which was deemed a draw, as both sides disputed the outcome.

As a result of that brief account, Neath are held to be the most senior of Welsh clubs, a title they cherish; because while the footballers of Swansea enjoyed a flirtation with the association game, the men of Neath stuck firmly with the rugger cause.

Rugby increased in popularity as the railway system expanded and the WFU introduced the South Wales Challenge Cup to ignite inter-town rivalry. Neath lost finals in 1880 and 1884 to Newport, but rugby had taken a grip on the town. The club spread its wings to take on English clubs like Bristol, Northampton and the exiles of London Welsh, and by the 1890s they were recognised as being Wales 'fifth' club, behind Cardiff, Llanelly, Newport and Swansea.

Under Bill Jones the club were determined to prove themselves and, by the turn of the century, Neath were ready to challenge that mighty group. With Wales enjoying its first 'Golden Era', in 1909/10 and 1910/11 centre Frank Rees led his charges to the very top – and after paying their first visit to France, where they beat Stade Français 11-3 in 1911, Neath even ran the 1912 Springboks mightily close.

The industrial terror of the First World War brought things to a halt, and Neath took time to adjust afterwards – although three annual games against the Barbarians saw them undefeated. Eventually, Tom Evans led them to the title again in 1928/29 and, despite a host of rugby league defections, Neath were champions again in 1933/34 and 1934/35, before war clouds gathered again in 1939.

This first volume is dedicated to the rise of Neath rugby from its earliest beginnings through to the Second World War, and to those who made it all happen – players, administrators and supporters. To one brought up on a steady diet of the wondrous deeds of 'Mourners' of yester-year, it is difficult to sum up Neath's contribution to the Welsh game. As this publication will show, Neath were the first club, Neath was the venue for the first meeting of the Welsh Football Union and Neath were the first to break the monopoly of the 'Big Four' – but facts are one thing, reputation another.

Neath's standing is perhaps best illustrated by a tale told to me by a long-term Neath adherent who, on being commissioned during the Second World War, was summoned to London to receive his posting. Upon discovering where our recruit was from, the commanding officer said, 'Ah! Neath – the place where all the best forwards come from'. This is a tradition which holds true today, and I can think of no finer testimony as to how the club is viewed from parts far afield.

Mike Price
July 2002

Acknowledgements

Any work of this nature owes an awful lot to the many people who assisted in its publication. Firstly, my thanks go to the modern-day board of Neath RFC for granting access to all records and permission to use their extensive clubhouse collection. From the outset, Alan Williams of Neath RFC has been very helpful and is a worthy successor to long-serving former committee-man Ken Davies as 'keeper of the club collection'.

In fact, this work would have been impossible without the dedication of Ken Davies, because it was he who first collated many of the photographs used. The images produced by a succession of cameramen from Messrs E. Moseley and Harry Jones in the early days through to H.G. Lewis and (more recently) Jim Giddings and Glyn Davies really bring to life the record of Neath RFC.

That I have been able to add the words and (hopefully!) tie things together into some kind of perspective has been a privilege: it has been a fascinating project.

My thanks go to the staff at Neath Reference Library (particularly Claire Smith and Jackie Thomas), to their counterparts at Swansea Central, Bridgend and Cardiff libraries, and to the archives department of Neath Port Talbot County Borough Council. All were very helpful (to say nothing of patient) in putting up with my endless demands for back copies of newspapers.

David Evans (*South Wales Evening Post*) and Fay Harris (*Neath Guardian*) kindly permitted the reproduction of newspaper articles and I am very grateful too to Mr Malcolm Thomas, the Neath Antiquarian Society and to all those who have kindly loaned scrapbooks and photographs which have helped make this unique record.

Finally, my thanks go to Becky Gadd and Kate Wiseman of Tempus Publishing for their guidance throughout the production of this publication.

Mike Price
September 2002

One
The Birthplace of Welsh Rugby

Dr T.P. Whittington, Neath's first captain, pictured later in life. Tom Whittington was also Neath's first international, representing Scotland against England in 1873 (although the records of the SRU list him as being from 'Merchiston', the famous Edinburgh academy).

The famous print depicting cricket at The Gnoll in 1862. Although this predates Neath rugby by a decade, it is unlikely that the setting would have changed much in the intervening years. Writing in 1937, Sam Clarke, Neath's first Welsh international, recalled playing at The Gnoll when he first came to the town in 1874; this is the background against which he would have played.

The earliest Neath team group, dated around 1873. The captain in front with the ball is Dr T.P. Whittington. Interestingly, only fourteen players are pictured – maybe the fifteenth was the early photographer?

FOOTBALL.

THE SOUTH WALES CHALLENGE CUP
LLANDILO v. NEATH match in the first tie of the South Wales Challenge Cup was played at Neath on Thursday. The Neath club scored eight touchdowns and five ties to nothing. Llandilo kicked off at 2 p.m., and time was called at 3.45. The Llandilo team were out-matched in weight and men, although the selection of players on the Neath side was the subject of strong comment on the field among those gentlemen who had practised with the club for the occasion, who were most invidiously excluded from the list in favour of the committee's friends. The play was not equal to the first contested tie on the same ground, the ball being kept within the Llandilo territory through the whole contest, making the match exceedingly one-sided.

FOOTBALL.

NEATH v. LLANELLY.—This football match was played on Saturday on the ground of the latter. The game was evenly contested throughout, Neath eventually winning by one goal and two touchdowns to one touchdown.

FOOTBALL FIXTURES.

Dec. 20 South Wales v. West of England.	Hereford
Dec. 20 Roath v. Aberdare	Aberdare
Dec. 21 Neath v. Swansea	Swansea
Dec. 22 Roath v. 10th G. R. V.	Cardiff
Dec. 26 Town v. Suburbs	Newport
Dec. 28 Swansea v. Brecon	Swansea
Dec. 29 Rockleaze v. Newport	Newport
Jan. 5 Cardiff v. Swansea	Swansea
Jan. 5 Cardiff 10th Rifles v. Newport	Cardiff
Jan. 10 Pegler's F. C. v. Cardiff 10th Rifles	Pontypool
Jan. 12 South Wales v. Clifton	Newport
Jan. 19 Cardiff v. Newport	Newport
Jan. 24 Swansea v. Newport	Swansea
Jan. 24 Blaenavon v. Pontypool	Blaenavon
Jan. 26 Swansea v. Llanelly	Swansea
Jan. 26 Cardiff v. Rockleaze	Cardiff
Feb. 9 Cardiff v. Cheltenham College	Cheltenham
Feb. 9 Cardiff 10th Rifles v. Ely	Ely
Feb. 14 Pontypool v. Newport Fifteen	Pontypool
Feb. 14 Pegler's F. C. v. Newport	Pontypool
Feb. 16 Cardiff v. Rockleaze	Bristol
Feb. 21 Pontypool v. Newport	Pontypool

Neath's first-ever Cup game. Llandeilo supplied the opposition in 1876, but Neath were comfortable winners. Fortified by the return of their captain Tom Whittington, Neath beat Llanelli in the next round, but lost to Swansea at the semi-final stage. The South Wales Challenge Cup excited great interest in the game in Wales. Neath never won the Cup but did reach two finals, losing to Newport on both occasions. In 1878/9, they fought an amazing sequence of seven games with Swansea; all resulted in draws until Neath emerged victorious thanks to a Beth Heycock try.

The Castle Hotel, Neath, birthplace of the WRU in March, 1881. Strangely, Neath were not listed among those clubs present at the launch. It has been suggested that Neath were not in favour of an All-Wales Union, preferring to stand by the South Wales (i.e. Glamorgan) Football Club of which Sam Clarke was secretary. However, the final of the South Wales Challenge Cup was being played at Neath that day, so maybe the club's representatives were simply too busy organising the fixture. Local opinion holds that Neath's attendance was simply 'taken as read', because the club had certainly been present one year earlier at Swansea, when the notion of an All-Wales Union was first mooted.

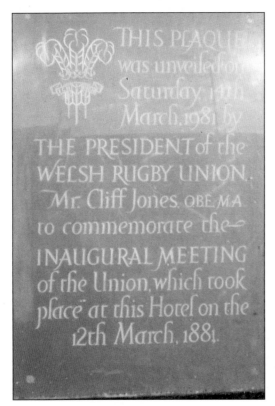

The plaque erected by the WRU to mark its centenary, which was unveiled by president Cliff Jones in 1981.

Forward P.J. (Phil) Braine emigrated to Australia in the early 1880s. The Maltese Cross (strictly a Cross forme) has gone through several variations during Neath's long history: Braine favoured this large version, which practically covered the whole of his jersey's front. E.C. Moxham is credited with having brought the Maltese Cross to Neath, worn it on his cap, and the team adopted it to break up the monotony of their early colours of 'assorted dark guernseys.' Legend has it that All Black became Neath's colours after the tragic death of one of its players, Dick Gordon, following injuries suffered playing against Bridgend on 7 February 1880.

Sam Clarke joined Neath in 1874, and was one of the leading Welsh rugby figures of his time. A strong advocate of the South Wales Football Club, it is said that the personal emnity between Clarke and Richard Mullock of Newport led to Neath's absence from the inaugural WFU meeting at the Castle Hotel. Whatever the case, the rift was healed and Clarke became the club's first Welsh international in 1882, and captained the club for three seasons from 1885/86, 1886/87 and 1887/88.

13

The transcript of the illuminated address presented to Sam Clarke on his departure from Neath in September 1888. Clarke moved to Wiltshire, where he represented his new county in football, hockey and cricket. Note the joint-secretaries – A. Russell Thomas, a local solicitor and former half back, became Mayor of Neath and was presented to Queen Victoria in her jubilee in 1897, while Walter E. Rees became secretary of the WFU.

A Neath team group from 1888/89, with H.A. Bowen as captain. Bowen was something of a rugby visionary, and was keen to see Neath spread their wings. He promoted games against English opposition including Hull and Wigan, and led Neath on a northern tour which saw them play six games in seven days over Christmas 1889. His foresight was not shared by the Neath Committee however, and after being called to account for his actions he joined Swansea.

Dr E. Vernon Pegge captained Neath from 1889 to 1892. The Briton Ferry doctor took over from Bowen, and shared his ideas for developing the game. So keen was he to accompany his side on their Devon tour in 1890 that when medical duties prevented him travelling with the team, he apocryphally hired his own train! Pegge played for Wales in 1891, but disappeared from the rugby scene in 1892.

Of the many characters produced by the Neath club, few can have exercised as much authority and influence over rugby affairs as Walter E. Rees. He served the Neath club as secretary and treasurer, and on becoming secretary of the WFU in 1896 held the office for a remarkable fifty-two years, until 1948.

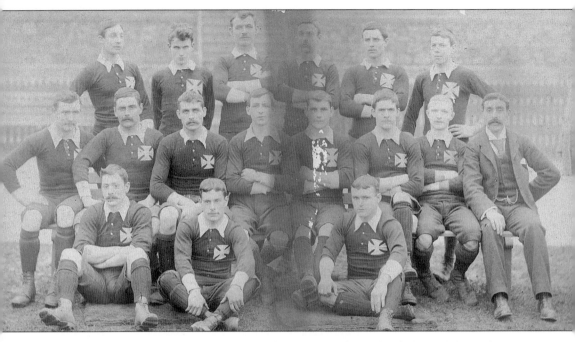

George D. Trick captained Neath in 1892/93 and 1893/94. 'The darling of the Melyn' was a local butcher, and he sliced through many a defence to score numerous tries from the right wing position. His team of 1892/3 includes, from left to right, back row: Mog Reynolds, Johnnie Williams, Fred Hutchinson, David Evans, Jack Brooks, Jim Davies. Middle row: Bill Jones, Howel Jones, John Edwards, George Trick (captain), Tom Thomas, Jim Thomas, Griff Lewis, Walter E. Rees (secretary). Front row: W.B. Morgan, Alec Cross, Wat Thomas.

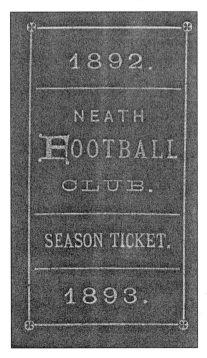

A Neath fixture card from 1892/93.

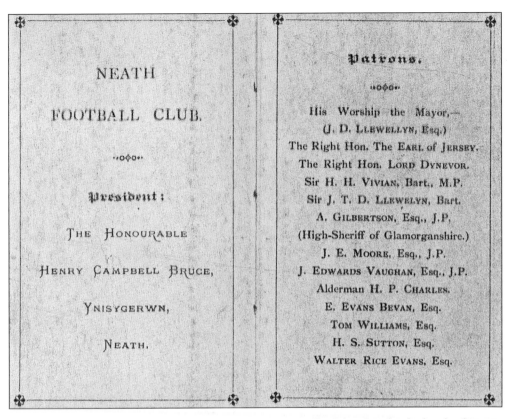

Neath RFC, like most clubs, was indebted to many well-off local individuals who became patrons of the game. This is a list of patrons from the 1892/93 season.

From its early days, Neath fielded a Second or 'A' XV; and they enjoyed a full fixture list in 1892/93. The 'A' team won the South Wales Challenge Cup in 1895, when the 'first-class' teams (as they had become known) were barred from the competition.

Month	Date	Opponent	Result			Venue
Sept.	17	Bristol	W	7	5	H
	24	Cardiff	W	7	6	H
Oct.	1	Penygraig	D	0	0	A
	3	Ulverston	L	5	7	H
	8	Aberavon	W	5	0	H
	15	Coventry	D	0	0	A
	22	Llanelly	D	0	0	A
	29	Lampeter College	W	6	2	H
Nov.	5	Penarth	L	4	5	A
	12	Aberavon	L	2	5	A
	19	Pontypridd	W	5	2	H
	26	Swansea	W	5	4	A
Dec.	3	*PROBABLES 14 pts POSSIBLES 5 pts (at Neath)*				
	10	Treorchy	W	11	0	H
	17	Cardiff	L	0	2	A
	24	Penygraig	W	10	0	H
	26	London Welsh	W	4	0	H
	27	Lancaster	C	-	-	H
	31	Morriston	C	-	-	H
Jan.	7	*WALES 12 pts ENGLAND 11 pts (at Cardiff)*				
	14	Llwynypia	W	11	0	H
	21	Swansea	L	0	2	A
	28	Morriston	D	0	0	A
Feb.	4	*SCOTLAND nil WALES 9 pts (at Raeburn Place)*				
	4	Cardiff Quins	W	7	6	H
	6	Aspull	L	6	7	H
	11	Pontypridd	L	0	4	A
	18	Llanelly	D	0	0	A
	25	Bristol	L	0	4	A
Mar.	4	Cardiff Quins	L	0	4	A
	11	*WALES 2 pts IRELAND nil (at Llanelly)*				
	11	Morriston	L	2	4	H
	18	Penarth	W	7	4	H
	25	Llanelly	D	0	0	A
	31	Cardiff & District	W	23	0	H
Apr.	1	Armley	W	7	0	H
	3	Morriston	W	12	7	H
	8	GWR XV	W	10	4	H
				156	**84**	

Played	**32**
Won	**16**
Drawn	**6**
Lost	**10**

Research has revealed the First XV results for 1892/93.

Neath RFC 1893/94. Trick's side finished with a record of Played 32, Won 15, Drawn 4, Lost 13, Points For 150, Points Against 114. From left to right, back row: J. Edwards, M. Reynolds, T. Thomas, D. Evans. Third row: W.E. Rees (secretary), A. Hutchinson, F. Hutchinson, J. Reynolds, H. Jones. Second row: H. Jones, W.G. Taylor, W. Thomas, C. Steer, G. Lewis. Front row: A. Cross, G.D. Trick (captain), W. Jones.

An artist's impression of the WFU Committee Badge belonging to Walter E. Rees – a family heirloom inherited by the author!

Left: Fred Hutchinson, capped by Wales in 1894, was a forward and railway worker from Briton Ferry. *Right:* Half back Alec Cross was one of the first to join Neath from outside the district. Like Hutchinson, he was a railway worker and hailed from Whitland.

Left: Cross' usual partner was Wat Thomas, one of five brothers to play for Neath. Thomas and Cross often exchanged positions, and had an uncanny understanding of each other's play. Wat Thomas was said to have kept himself fit by running from his Melyn home along the canal bank to work in Aberdulais. *Right:* Centre Charlie Steer captained Neath in 1894/95 and 1895/96, and appeared regularly until the turn of the century.

NEATH v. PENARTH.

For the second time this season Neath met Penarth. On the former occasion the White and Blacks journeyed to the Cardiff suburb, and, notwithstanding a really good display of football, the visitors were defeated by four tries to nil. It was anticipated and devoutly to be hoped that the Seasiders would not have so much to their credit to go away with on Saturday Accordingly the homesters made arrangements for a tough battle, and both teams were fairly well represented, as the subjoined will show :— The ground was in anything but good condition ; it was, however, in that state which the players in both teams are very well acquainted with.

The teams were :

POSITION.	NEATH.	PENARTH.
Back	Joe Davies	Clemence
Three-quarter	W. Jones	J. Alexander
Three-quarter	J. Williams	H. Morgan
Three-quarter	C. Steer	Garrett
Three-quarter	J. Griffiths	Angove
Half-back	Wat Thomas	Hutchings
Half-back	A. Cross	Dewar
Forward	F. Hutchinson	Ellis
Forward	A. Hutchinson	Jackson
Forward	G. Lewis	Morris
Forward	M. Reynolds	Evans
Forward	H. Jones	J. Matthews
Forward	J. Thomas	W. Matthews
Forward	J. Brooks	Landry
Forward	J. Edwards	Varner

Referee : Mr. Nicholl, Cardiff.

The visitors were late. Penarth kicked off, and a good return was made by the home custodian, and from a scrum in the centre Cross dashed off, and punted down to the visitors' quarters. Play was soon transferred, however, to mid-field again, where Neath were penalised for offside play. The kick availed the Penarth men but little, and again the homesters came into their quarters. But with the combined play of the Suburbans the game was transferred to Neath territory, where Steers returned the leather to the centre. Here some hard scrummaging followed. At this point the home quartet participated in a rare passing bout, and looked like scoring, but the oval was lost. Penarth was next penalised, and Joe Davies, from a favourable position, took a kick for goal, the ball dropping immediately underneath the Penarth uprights, a minor resulting. Play of an exciting character followed, neither side gaining much advantage Action for a time hovered about the centre, where Penarth were again penalised, and a strong kick took play into the visitors' territory, where the Neath men remained for a time. The Suburbans were again penalised, but Joe Davies' kick did not cover much ground. Scrimmages followed, the leather coming out frequently, and was handled by the visitors' three-quarters in a most clumsy manner.

The result was they made little headway with all their chances. Garrett could not shine at all, and his runs were of the briefest description. Steers and Jack Edwards, for Neath, played a marvellously good game, as did also Bill Jones. The last-named, picking up smartly on one occasion, passed to his confrere, and Williams, making away finely, was only collared on the visitors' line. Relief, however, came, and the battle waged in front of the Penarth goal. Garrett here picked up, and Herbert Morgan, ceiving the pass, made away splendidly, but was beautifully collared by Joe Davies. Hostilities were then taken to the centre, but eventually transferred to the home twentyfive, but all attempts to break down the defence offered were futile. The visitors now hardly pressed their opponents, and Dick Garrett putting in a strong kick the leather went over the homesters' line, and they were compelled to concede a minor. Half-time was then called, the score being—

Penarth—2 minors
Neath—1 minor

During the second half the homesters for the most part held a decided advantage. At no time did Penarth look really dangerous. Operations had not been commenced for more than ten minutes before one of a series of brilliant bouts of passing engaged in by the Neath quartet resulted in Bill Jones nearly getting over, and a minute later Clemens picked up near his own line and was charged, and Jack Griffiths, obtaining possession, trotted over with a try, and this Alec Cross easily converted. During the last ten minutes of the game the defence of the visitors was taxed to the utmost. Three times did the Neath men almost cross their opponents' line, and when time was called the score stood :—

Neath—1 goal, 3 minors.
Penarth—3 minors.

Remarks on the Game.

The battle was an exceedingly tough one, and brought out the merits of each team to the greatest possible advantage. It was seen early in the game, however, that the visitors were not going to have matters all their own sweet way, for the homesters retaliated with a vigour and promptness that at once impressed their opponents that in the event of their going down it would be to anything but the tune they received when they previously met the Seasiders on their own heath. The first half was desperately fought out, every inch of ground that was gained by sheer hard work. In the second half, however, the visitors fell away in a most remarkable way, and their efforts were of the feeblest character. They played a fairly good defensive game, and Edwards' try was secured very trickily, and Cross converted very neatly. Taking all in all, the best team were undoubtedly the visitors.

By the 1890s, comprehensive match reports were appearing in local newspapers, as shown by these descriptions of Neath's 3-0 revenge win over Penarth on January 19 1895.

Played at the now called Fair Field
NEATH
with Rosser St in the background

NEATH v SWANSEA. 1895.
The first match in which **NEATH** were beaten on their
own ground.

The earliest known photograph of Neath in action, dated 20 April 1895. Swansea are the visitors, who won 3-0; the venue is the old Bird-in-Hand Field, where Neath had temporarily moved to following a dispute with the landlords of The Gnoll. The backs of the houses in Rosser Street shown here are still clearly discernible today. This was the first game Neath lost on The Bird-in-Hand Field, which later became the home for the town's famous September Fair. The site is now occupied by Neath Civic Centre.

> *"O, Charlie Steer*
> *You are a dear,*
> *Your face is sweet And I love to hear*
> *The patter of your big feet !"*

In the 1890s, newspapers often carried humorous verses regarding the Welsh game. This effort 'in praise' of Charlie Steer appeared in 1895, and was said to have been contributed by a lady supporter of the 'Black Brigade' – although the author suspects that the mischievous hand of a fellow Neath player may have been at work.

Two

Bill Jones – from controversy to challengers

Bill Jones, Neath RFC 1891-1909: if any individual was synonymous with Neath RFC as the club 'came of age', it was he. Jones joined Neath in 1890 as a winger, but 'on account of failing eye-sight' he found his way into the pack! He is officially listed as having captained Neath for some nine seasons. His accession was by no means straightforward however, as despite being the popular choice in 1896/97, 'the Melyn faction' on the committee instead appointed Second XV captain Tom Powell. So deeply hurt was Jones that he led a mass boycott carried out by his backers. Neath struggled as a consequence, until Powell stood down in January. By the end of the season Jones was in command, and dedicated himself to the All Black cause. He skippered for the next two seasons, resumed again in 1900/01 and 1901/02, and finished off with a four-year stint from 1905/06 to 1908/09. In recognition of his outstanding service, he was popularly elected the club's first Life Member after Neath won their first championship in 1909/10.

Neath RFC, 1896/97. This end-of-season photograph has Bill Jones happily restored to the captaincy. From left to right, back row: W.G. Taylor, A. Moxley, M. Reynolds, E. Arnold, H. Jones. Middle row: D.J. Price (secretary), S. Davies, J. Linnard, D. Evans, J. Davies, C. Morris, J. Edwards. Front row: J. Thomas, G. Lewis, W. Jones (captain), A. Hopkins, C. Powell, H. Hanford.

Jim Reynolds was a stalwart Neath forward of the 1890s. He led the team after Tom Powell stood down, before handing over to Bill Jones. Reynolds (at thirteen and a half stones, one of the heaviest forwards of the time) and Evan Vigors are believed to have been the first Neath players to go north to Rugby League when they joined Swinton in 1898.

Full-back Joe Davies was reserve to the great W.J. Bancroft on no fewer than 17 occasions, and he would surely have been capped in any other era. During the Powell crisis he played a season for Llanelli, but immediately returned to Neath once peace was restored, and led the Blacks in 1899/1900.

J.D.D. Davis was a prolific wing three-quarter. Jack 'Brynheulog' (named after his house) scored the last try at the Bird-in-Hand Field against Pontypridd in 1898, and harvested a record 25 points (5 tries and 5 conversions) for the Seconds against Tondu in 1897.

Griff Lewis (above left) and Evan Arnold (above right) were stalwart forwards who both served Neath for nearly a decade.

Alf Moxley joined from Pontypool and established himself in the Neath pack, but arguably his greatest service to the club came later – he was grandfather of the Wales and Lions line-out ace Roy John.

Fair-haired Harry Jones was a try-scoring centre, who took over Charlie Steer's mantle in the Neath midfield.

Left: Bill Carney was a typical hard-working forward, who sadly retired early in 1905 due to a bad leg injury. The club organised a benefit game for him.

Right: D.J. Rosser was another worthy forward who rendered yeoman service for a decade, interrupted only by a short break from the game when he, along with Bill Jones and Idris Jones, succumbed to the great religious revival. He soon returned to action.

Left: Half-back Jack Phillips was rarely guaranteed a regular place. He usually did duty for the Seconds, but was never found wanting when called upon by the seniors.

Below left: T.R. (Tom) Thomas was a regular in the Neath pack up until 1914. During this time, the Neath pack became known as the 'Terrible Eight' of Welsh club rugby.

Below right: Tom Reason was another reliable member of the Neath pack from 1902 to 1911.

Bill Jones captained Neath in 1900/01, and the team are pictured prior to a match at The Gnoll. In the front row is utility back Willie Arnold, who top-scored with 15 tries, but was tempted away to Llanelli, and was later capped in Wales' 6-0 defeat by Scotland in 1903. From left to right, back row: C. Powell, N. Moore, J. Linnard, D.H. Davies, W.G. Taylor, Howel Jones, H. Hopes, A. Moxley, W. Jenkins, A.W.M. Tench (secretary). Middle row: W. Hodges (trainer), T. Davies, H. Hanford, A. Hopkins, W. Jones (captain), Joe Davies, Harry Jones, Dan Davies. Front row: C. Morris, W.R. Arnold, L. Jenkins, E. Arnold.

D.J. Price succeeded Walter Rees as secretary.

Bill Jones was captain again in 1901/02.

Neath Excelsiors reached the final of the South Wales Challenge Cup in 1901/02, but lost to (Aber)Cynon Stars in the final. The players received medals as pictured from WFU secretary Walter E. Rees.

Fred David was a real stalwart of the Neath club. He started playing with Neath Excelsiors (virtually Neath Seconds), and soon became a durable, reliable forward. Fred David captained Neath in 1912/13 and later became chairman and the club's second life member.

D.H. Davies (back row, bare arms) won his only Welsh cap against Scotland at Swansea on 6 February 1904. Despite Wales winning 21-3, he was omitted from the next game! He was also a cricketer of local repute, and later served on the WFU where his wisdom was appreciated by all. His passion for rugby and sporting fair play is perhaps best illustrated by the fact that when on the WFU in 1927, he proposed that Wales should take a team to play Cross Keys in order to raise funds for the home club, who had been financially stricken by the after-effects of the General Strike. His idea was taken up, and Wales sent virtually a full XV (including Neath's Emrys Jones, Tom Arthur and Tom Hollingdale). They lost 13-3 – but Cross Keys had been saved.

D.H. Davies was captain in 1902/03. He took the unprecedented step of making a public apology for his team's home defeat by Swansea on 24 January 1903 – despite the fact that he himself was injured and unable to play.

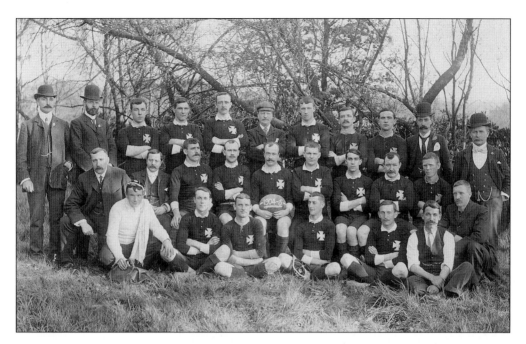

Howel Jones took over as captain in 1904/05.

Neath RFC, 1905/06 captained by Howel Jones. From left to right, back row: J.E. Jones (chairman), J.R. Griffiths (committee), Evan Arnold, D.J. Rosser, Henry Hopes, Tom Jones (treasurer), Fred David (vice-captain), D.H. Davies, Tom Lloyd, Tom Reason, A.L. David (secretary), Walter Gabriel (committee). Middle row: George John, R.K. Green, Bill Jones, Chris Hendra, Howel Jones (captain), William Bevan, Sam Abraham, Tom Thomas, David Davies, J.S. Mills (committee), D. Davies (committee). Front: George Doran (trainer), R.T. Davies, Idris Jones, Tom Jones, Johnnie Thomas, Tom Davies, A.G. Parker, Alf Moxley (committee).

Howel Jones (brother of Bill) was an outstanding athlete, and like his brother he had the capacity to play both inside and outside the scrum. He established a new First XV record when he scored 5 tries and kicked 3 conversions against Treherbert on Easter Monday 1906 – his try record stood until beaten by his son Howie, who scored six against Aberavon in 1928/29. Howel Jones was capped by Wales at forward in Wales' 14-12 defeat in Belfast in 1904.

A general view of Neath in the early 1900s, showing both cricket and rugby fields. Note the stand and terracing on Gnoll Park Road and, inside the ropes, the seating around the perimeter.

Neath RFC, 1906/07. From left to right, back row: Dan Davies, T.C. Lloyd, W.J. Perry, F.W. David, D.H. Davies, T.J. Reason, R.K. Green, H. Hopes, W. Sandham. Middle row: W.B. Morgan (chairman), W.M. Edwards, H. Merriman, Howel Jones, W. Jones (captain), J.D.D. Davis, R.T. Davies, R. Phillips, T.R. Thomas, A.L. David (secretary). Front row: G. Dorey (trainer), T.J. (Shon) Evans, J. Brennan, J. Thomas.

Joe Burchill was a fine outside half who played for Neath and Glamorgan County. He joined the club from Swansea Excelsiors and was a Welsh travelling reserve; but the cumbersome Welsh selection system was not interested in Neath backs, and Burchill went north to play for Hull.

Forward Ned Lee.

Ned Lee and centre Gwilym Jones (right) were two underrated but very essential cogs in the 'mould breakers' of 1909/10.

Johnnie Thomas was an efficient scrum worker for Neath at the turn of the century.

T.J. ('Shon') Evans played scrum-half for Neath in the early 1900s. He was at his best when confronted by the inter-national players like Dicky Owen (Swansea) and Tommy Vile (Newport), who limited him to a place as Wales' travel-ling reserve; few enjoyed playing against him. After the war, he became the club's trainer and enjoyed Neath's inter-war successes.

Mr Arthur L. David succeeded Mr D.J. Price as secretary. His reign of office encompassed Neath's pre-war rise, and he was instrumental in getting the All Blacks restarted after the war.

Neath had two players by the name of Tom Davies in their back division during the early 1900s. The first (left) debuted in 1899 and was a free-scoring wing. He became trainer immediately after the First World War. The second Tom Davies, known as 'Tom Tit', was a utility back.

Three
Breaking the Mould

Bill Jones had set about making Neath a power in the Welsh game, as they sought to break the monopoly of the 'Big Four' of Cardiff, Llanelli, Newport and Swansea. The Gnoll was becoming an intimidating arena in which to play, and Neath RFC boasted a ground record in 1907/08: Played 32, Won 23, Drawn 3, Lost 6. From left to right, back Row: W. Gabriel, Jonah Arnold (treasurer), H. Hopes, T.C. Lloyd, W.J. Perry, T.J. Reason, Rees Phillips, D.R. Edwards. Middle row: Standing: J.S. Mills (vice chairman), J.B. Williams, D. Jones, Rev. A.E.C. Morgan, J.D.D. Davies, Howel Jones, D.H. Davies, W. Sandham, F.W. David, F.E. Taylor, A.L. David (secretary), J. Morris. Front row: H. Merriman (trainer), R.T. Davies, T. Thomas, W.B. Morgan (chairman), W. Jones (captain), W.M. Edwards, C. Powell, G. Hopes. Front row: Frank Rees, J.R. Phillips, J. Brennan, Johnnie Thomas, T. Davies, Shon Evans.

Cardiff found Neath a particularly hard nut to crack at The Gnoll. This cartoon marks a Blue and Blacks failure on 8 February 1908, when Neath won 5-3.

The cartoonists had a field day as the chase for the championship intensified.

Neath had a very respectable record against the 'Welsh Metropolitans', as Cardiff were called. In 1908 however, the Arms Park saw the final appearance of Howel Jones. He left the field with an injury which was diagnosed as being to do with his rib, and then as appendicitis, before finally doctors operated to remove a tumour in his liver. He was so weakened by the operation that he passed away, and Neath lost one of its finest players.

Howel Jones' team-mates attended his funeral, and the match against Merthyr on 3 December was cancelled as a mark of respect.

NEATH FOOTBALL CLUB.

CADOXTON, NEATH,

December 2nd, 1908.

Dear Sir,

In consequence of the lamented death of our sincere friend, Mr. HOWEL JONES, the match with Merthyr, on Saturday next, has been Postponed. The Funeral will take place on FRIDAY NEXT, leaving Neath at **12** o'clock for Pont-neath-vaughan. The Committee earnestly hope that you will make every effort possible to attend the Funeral, and pay your last respect to your old Comrade and fellow Footballer.

Conveyances will be provided for the journey to Pont-neath-vaughan. It has been decided to meet at the "Bird-in-Hand" on Friday morning at 11.30 sharp.

If you are unable to attend the Funeral, kindly let me hear from you immediately.

Yours faithfully,

ARTHUR L. DAVID.

The third Jones brother, Idris, played centre three-quarter for Neath. Although his service was not quite as distinguished as that of his brothers, many rated him the most talented of the three.

The Australian tour party of 1908/09, captained by Dr H.M. Moran. Pictured bottom left is D.B. (Danny) Carroll, at nineteen the youngest member of the touring party. Carroll turned out for Neath in their 13-3 Boxing Day win over London Welsh, who themselves included three of the tourists – McIntyre, Craig and Daly.

Neath combined with Aberavon to take on a touring team for the first time in October 1908. The combined side lost 15-0; this sequence of photos shows six scenes from the game.

45

R.K. (Bob) Green was a member of the Anglo-Welsh XV which toured New Zealand in 1908. Green, a surveyor, came to Neath to work, and he soon became a key member of their robust eight. He left the town between the wars to take up a post with the water authority in the south of England.

W.M. Edwards was an excellent goal-kicking full back for Neath in 1907/08. A postman in Aberkenfig, he was a Welsh reserve but joined the Northern Union side Huddersfield in 1908, and so missed out on Neath's assault on the championship.

The Neath club ran trips for the players to internationals at Cardiff. These arrangements were made for the Wales-Australia game in December 1908.

NEATH FOOTBALL CLUB.

Cadoxton, Neath,

December 7th, 1908.

Dear Sir,

Australia v. Wales at Cardiff,

December 12th, 1908.

IT has been arranged that the Committee and Players of this Club should witness the above Match on SATURDAY NEXT. The Party will travel to Cardiff by the Excursion train leaving Neath at 12.10.

Tickets for Inside the Ropes for the Match will be provided each member of the Party.

After the Match, the Committee and Players will dine together at the "Philharmonic Restaurant," St. Mary Street, at 5 o'clock sharp.

The Party will return from Cardiff at 10.25.

If you are unable to attend, kindly let me know BY RETURN OF POST, to enable me to make arrangements accordingly.

Yours faithfully,

ARTHUR L. DAVID,

Secretary.

Bill Jones led Neath for the last time in 1908/09. Here the 'Mourners', as they were now called (due to their black jerseys, and the tragic death of Howel Jones following that of Dick Gordon), are pictured before a game at a packed Gnoll. Their record was: Played 35, Won 27, Drawn 2 and Lost 6 with 387 Points For and 83 Against.

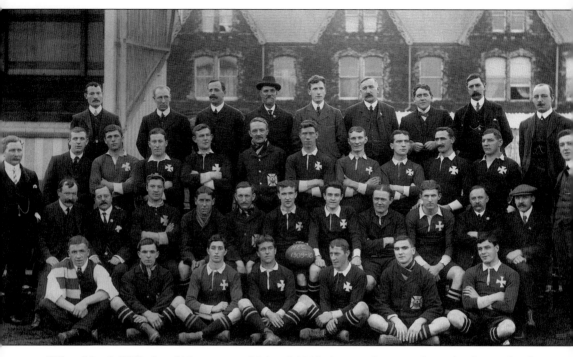

When Neath RFC played Newport on 16 April 1910, the match was acclaimed as being 'for the Welsh championship'. Neath won the match 4-3, but Newport claimed that Neath's fixture list was not as strong as theirs (matches with Llanelli and Swansea had been suspended due to rough play) and that, beaten or not, they were the champions. However there was no doubt in Neath who were the champions, as Frank Rees and his men enjoyed the wonderful record in 1909/10 of Played 37, Won 31, Drawn 4, Lost 2, Points For 429 Points Against 85. Pictured are the 'mould breakers of Welsh rugby'. From left to right, back row: C. Powell, F.E. Taylor, J.D.D. Davies, G. Hopes, D. Jones, W. Gabriel, J.B. Williams, A.L. David (secretary), H. David. Third row: J.S. Mills, D. Richards, E.J. Lee, H. Davies, T.C. Lloyd, D.H. Davies (chairman), W.J. Perry, T.T Jenkins, T.J. Reason, J. Pullman, F.W. David. Second row: W. Jones (vice captain), W.B. Morgan, T.R. Thomas, A. Williams, T. Davies, F. Rees (captain), T.E. John, R.K. Green, G. Jones, J. Morris, D.R. Edwards, J. Arnold (treasurer). Front row: H. Merriman (trainer), T.T. Davies, Edgar Thomas, J. Brennan, J. Thomas, D. Parry, T.J. Evans.

Fred Rees was a star 'find' for Neath in 1910/11. The former Swansea full back only played one season for the Blacks, but in that time he made quite an impact.

		SEASON 1909/10		CAPTAIN : FRANK REES		
Sept.	4	Neath District League	W	17	6	H
	11	Ystalyfera	W	22	5	H
	18	Leicester	L	5	13	A
	20	Coventry	D	0	0	A
	25	Glamorgan Police	W	21	0	H
Oct.	2	Pill Harriers	W	17	0	H
	9	Aberavon	W	10	0	A
	16	Ammanford	W	37	0	H
	23	Plymouth Albion	W	9	6	A
	30	Pontypool	W	8	0	H
Nov.	6	Newport	W	0	0	A
	13	Lydney	W	15	3	A
	20	Bridgend	W	10	5	A
	27	Aberavon	W	9	5	H
Dec.	4	Cardiff	W	3	0	A
	11	Skewen	C	-	-	A
	18	Briton Ferry	W	31	0	H
	25	Bridgend	W	8	4	H
	27	Ebbw Vale	W	6	0	H
	28	Brynmawr	W	6	0	H
Jan.	1	WALES 49 pts FRANCE 14 pts (at Swansea)				
	8	Aberavon	W	13	4	A
	15	ENGLAND 11 pts WALES 6 pts (at Twickenham)				
	15	Penygraig	W	8	0	H
	22	Bridgend	W	7	3	A
	29	Treorchy	W	6	0	H
Feb.	5	WALES 14 pts SCOTLAND nil (at Cardiff)				
	12	Gloucester	W	14	3	H
	14	Leicester	W	11	0	H
	19	Lydney	W	3	0	A
	26	Cardiff	W	5	4	H
	28	Coventry	W	9	3	H
Mar.	5	Pontypool	D	0	0	A
	12	IRELAND 3 pts WALES 19 pts (at Dublin)				
	12	Aberavon	W	9	4	H
	19	London Welsh	L	6	8	A
	26	Gloucester	D	0	0	A
	28	Cwmbran	W	25	6	H
Apr.	2	Bridgend	W	38	0	H
	9	Llwynypia	W	22	0	H
	16	Newport	W	4	3	H
	23	Plymouth Albion	W	17	0	H
				431	85	

Played	37
Won	31
Drawn	4
Lost	2

WELSH CHAMPIONS - FIRST OCCASION

Notes
1 Newport disputed Neath's title claim as "fixtures cannot be compared"
2 4 wins over Aberavon - first time by either side in fixture
3 Llanelly and Swansea not played due to "rough play"
4 First fixture versus Gloucester

Neath RFC results, 1909/10.

Neath RFC retained the Welsh title in 1910/11. Their fine record was: Played 39, Won 32, Drawn 3, Lost 4, Points For 484 Points Against 68, and they extended their ground record to three seasons. From left to right, back row: D. Jones (vice chairman), P. Howells, J.B. Williams, W. Jones, T.C. Lloyd, D.H. Davies, J.Birch, G. Stephens, G. Hopes, F.E. Taylor. Third row: C. Powell, W.B. Morgan, H. Griffiths ('The Druid'), J.S. Mills, W. Gabriel, H. Merriman (trainer), J. Pullman, T.R. Thomas, T.J. Reason, W.J. Perry, T. Davies, F.W. David, D.R. Edwards, A.L. David (secretary). Second row: J. Thomas, T.T. Jenkins, R.K. Green, D. Parry, Frank Rees (captain), Fred Rees, Howel Davies, J. Morris. J. Arnold (treasurer). Front row: M. Lloyd, T.J. Evans, I. Jones, Edgar Thomas, T. John, J. Brennan.

Neath Football Club and Athletic Association.

SEASON 1910-11

Member's Ticket.

(For Admission to Club Matches only).

IMPORTANT NOTICE.

IN the event of a match being played which is not already included in the Fixture List, Members will be admitted to witness such match only on production of Ticket of Membership.

ARTHUR LL. DAVID,
Secretary.

NEATH PRINTING CO.

Welsh Football Union Fixtures.

1911.

January 21st—Wales v. England at Swansea.

February 4th—Scotland v. Wales at Edinburgh.

February 28th—France v. Wales at Paris.

March 11th—Wales v. Ireland at Cardiff.

A Neath RFC season ticket from 1910/11.

Sept.	3	Neath District League	W	13	0	H
	10	Pontypridd	W	9	0	H
	17	Leicester	L	0	3	A
	24	Bridgend	W	45	5	H
Oct.	1	Pill Harriers	W	11	0	H
	8	Aberavon	W	10	0	H
	15	Swansea	L	0	3	A
	22	Glamorgan Police	W	5	3	H
	29	Lydney	W	14	6	A
Nov.	5	Pontypridd	W	28	0	H
	12	Bridgend	W	16	0	A
	14	Leicester	W	23	3	H
	19	Newport	L	5	9	A
	26	Lydney	W	13	0	H
Dec.	3	Cardiff	L	0	11	A
	10	Bath	W	22	0	H
	17	Gloucester	C	-	-	H
	24	Edinburgh University	W	6	0	H
	26	Brynmawr	W	3	0	H
	27	London Irish	W	17	3	H
	31	Llwynypia	W	28	6	H
Jan.	7	Gloucester	W	5	3	A
	14	Bath	W	4	0	A
	21	*WALES 15 pts ENGLAND 11 pts (at Swansea)*				
	28	Aberavon	D	0	0	A
Feb.	4	*SCOTLAND 10 pts WALES 32 pts (at Inverleith)*				
	4	Mountain Ash	W	6	0	
	11	Pontypridd	D	0	0	H
	18	Cardiff	W	6	3	H
	25	Aberavon	W	10	0	A
	28	*FRANCE nil WALES 15 pts (at Paris)*				
Mar.	4	Pontypool	D	0	0	H
	11	*WALES 16 IRELAND nil (at Cardiff)*				
	18	Bridgend	W	8	0	A
	23	Stade Francais	W	11	3	A
	27	Treherbert	W	26	5	H
Apr.	1	Aberavon	W	3	0	A
	8	London Welsh	W	9	0	H
	14	Bridgend	W	19	3	H
	15	Headingley	W	18	0	H
	17	Belfast Collegians	W	19	3	H
	18	Ferndale	W	22	0	H
	22	Newport	W	3	0	H
				437	72	

Played	37
Won	31
Drawn	3
Lost	4

WELSH CHAMPIONS - SECOND OCCASION

Notes   1 *20-match invincible run from December 23rd.*
           2 *Ground Record preserved.*
           3 *Swansea re-instated.*
           4 *First "overseas" fixture at Stade Francais*
           5 *First Scottish side - Edinurgh University.*
           6 *Llanelly not played.*

Neath RFC results, 1910/11.

Joe Pullman was capped by Wales in their 49-14 win over France in January 1910, but was immediately dropped. He soldiered on for Neath, and although he was elected captain for 1914/15, the outbreak of the First World War denied him the chance to lead them.

PC (later Sgt) Bill Perry (back row, third from left) won his only cap in the Welsh XV that defeated England in January 1911. He was one of the mainstays of the Neath pack from 1905, and even appeared after the First World War, when well into his thirties. He later served on the Neath Committee.

Bill Perry was replaced in the Welsh pack by fellow Neath forward Jim Birch (back row, third from right), who was also a policeman and was based at Skewen. Birch played in the victories over Scotland and Ireland as Wales completed a Triple Crown victory in 1911.

Jack Brennan. The Brennans are a famous Neath rugby family and Jack played outside-half from 1906 to 1913, scoring 117 points in 1909/10. He later transferred to Maesteg, playing for the 'Men from the Plateau' against Neath in 1913/14.

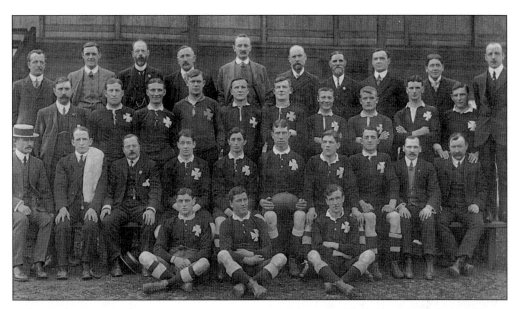

W.J. (Bill) Perry led Neath RFC in 1911/12. Although not quite as successful as in previous years, Neath were still a formidable team. From left to right, back row: W. Brennan, D.B. Williams, A.W.M. Tench, W. Gabriel, D.H. Davies, G. Hopkins, G. Hopes (vice chairman), P. Howells, J.B. Williams. Third row: A.L. David (secretary), Howell Davies, T.T. Jenkins, J. Birch, M. Lloyd, T.C. Lloyd, T.R. Thomas, Evan Davies, W. Hopkins, Fred David, Harry David. Second row: C. Powell, T. Evans (trainer), W.B. Morgan, G. Gethin, Edgar Thomas, W.J. Perry (captain), H. Richards, W. Davies, D.R. Edwards, W. Jones. Front row: T. Davies, J. Brennan, Frank Rees.

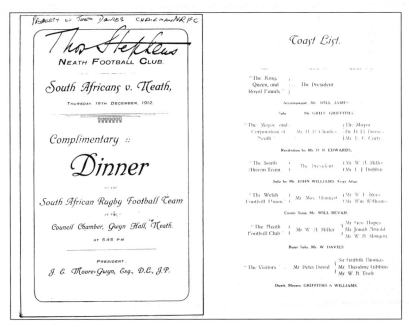

The menu card from Neath v. South Africa, December 1912. The extensive toast list kept the guests occupied long into the night.

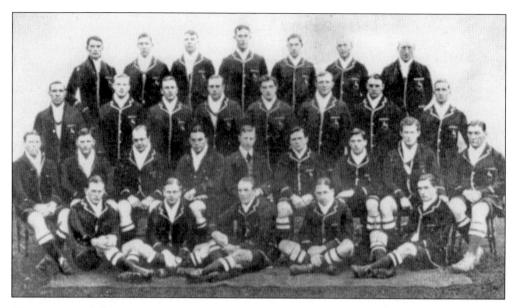

The 1912 South Africans were the first major touring team to be faced by Neath in their own right. They edged a stormy encounter at The Gnoll in December 1912 by 8-3. Handel Richards got Neath's try, but the South African press reacted every bit as hysterically to the game as they did some eighty years later.

In Memory of
Poor Old Springboks
Who were defeated by
GOOD OLD NEATH,
At Neath. Dec. 19th, 1912.

The Springboks may gallop. the Springboks may leap,
The Springboks may fine figures cut
Yet records unbroken are hard things to keep
For Welsh goats still know how to butt.

E. DAVIES & CO   PARADISE PLACE CARDIFF

Condolence cards were often produced to hail sporting upsets prior to the First World War. This marked Neath's great effort against the 1912 Springboks and celebrated Neath's 'moral' victory.

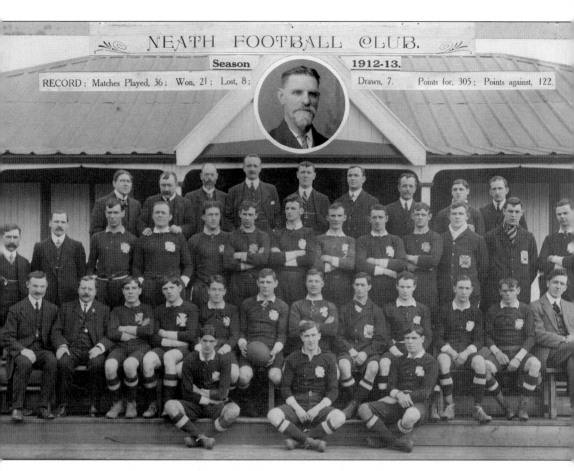

NEATH FOOTBALL CLUB.

Season		1912-13.

RECORD : Matches Played, 36 ; Won, 21 ; Lost, 8 ;   Drawn, 7.   Points for, 305 ; Points against, 122.

Neath RFC, 1912/13. Played 36, Won 21, Drawn 7, Lost 8, Points For 305, Points Against 122 – and they nearly beat the Springboks! From left to right, back row: J.B. Williams (vice chairman), W. Jones, A.W.M. Tench, D.H. Davies, Tom Stephens, P. Howells, W. Brennan, T. Davies, T. Evans (trainer). Third row: A.L. David (secretary), D.R. Edwards, D.M. Davies, R.K. Green, Fred Perrett, D. Jones, W. Hopkins, T.T. Jenkins, W. Davies, Geo. Rees, T.C. Lloyd, G. Stephens, Ben John. Second row: C. Powell, W.B. Morgan, Dai Morgan, H. Richards, G. Gethin, Fred David (captain), T.R. Thomas, Edgar Thomas, R. Stroud, Tommy Owen, T.O. Jones, J. Arnold (treasurer). Front row: Howel Davies, Frank Rees, T.J. Evans, G.Hopes (inset).

Two players of the 1912/13 team were to lose their lives in the First World War. Fred Perrett enjoyed a meteoric rise to fame in this period, his only season of first-class rugby. He joined Neath in September 1912 and represented club, Glamorgan County and Wales against South Africa before appearing in all of Wales' internationals of 1912/13. He then went north and joined the Royal Welsh Fusiliers, being commissioned as Second Lieutenant in 1917; he was wounded in one of the final actions of the war. He died of his wounds in December 1918, but his name does not appear in the WRU Roll of Honour (presumably because he joined the Rugby League).

Left: Winger Tommy Owen joined Neath from Resolven, and had attained the rank of sergeant when he was killed on the Western Front in 1916.

Right: Handel Richards, Neath's try-scorer against the 1912 Springboks.

Awaiting the cataclysm – Neath RFC 1913/14. Seven-times capped T.C. (Tom) Lloyd led Neath in their final pre-war season. From left to right, back row: A.E. Freethy, W. Gabriel, W. Jones, W. Brennan, H. Waring, A.W.M. Tench, D.H. Davies, M. Arnold, J. Pullman, T. Stephens, P. Howells. Third row: A.L. David (secretary), D.M. Davies, G. Stephens, A. Rees, W.J. Perry, W. Hopkins, Jack Jones, W. Davies, F.W. David, M. Lloyd, O. Hopkins. Second row: C. Powell (vice chairman), T. Evans (trainer), T.E. John, G. Gethin, L. Davies, T.C. Lloyd (captain), W. Adey, R. Stroud, T. Owen, J.B. Williams (Chairman), D.R. Edwards. Front row: R. Pritchard, E. Cornfield, D. Morgan, M. Rees, D. Hanford.

Frank Rees, who captained Neath to their first championship, played his final game in 1913.

Date		Opponent	Result	For	Against	H/A
Sept.	6	Glynneath	W	11	0	H
	13	Resolven	W	10	5	H
	20	Pill Harriers	W	9	0	A
	27	Pontypridd	W	17	0	H
Oct.	4	Aberavon	L	3	8	H
	11	Penarth	W	13	5	H
	18	Cardiff	L	3	9	A
	25	Llanelly	W	10	9	H
Nov.	1	Abertillery	L	0	9	A
	8	Newport	W	11	6	H
	15	Cardiff	L	0	4	A
	22	Devonport Services	W	20	0	H
	29	Swansea	W	7	0	A
Dec.	6	Northampton	C	-	-	H
	13	Bridgend	W	14	9	A
	20	Pontypool	D	3	3	
	25	London Welsh	W	15	9	H
	26	Abertillery	W	11	0	A
	27	Swansea	L	0	3	H
Jan.	3	Pontypridd	D	0	0	A
	10	Devonport Services	L	3	6	A
	12	Torquay Athletic	W	3	0	A
	17	*ENGLAND 10 pts WALES 9 pts (at Twickenham)*				
	17	Maesteg	W	5	3	H
	24	Llanelly	L	6	9	A
	31	Aberavon	L	3	8	A
Feb.	7	*WALES 24 pts SCOTLAND 5 pts (at Cardiff)*				
	14	Bridgend	W	13	0	H
	21	Swansea	L	0	8	H
	28	Mountain Ash	D	3	3	A
Mar.	2	*WALES 31 pts FRANCE nil (at Swansea)*				
	7	Pontypool	L	0	24	A
	14	*IRELAND 3 pts WALES 14 pts (at Belfast)*				
	14	Briton Ferry	C	-	-	H
	21	Bridgend	W	9	3	A
	26	Glamorgan Police	W	21	0	H
	28	Penarth	D	0	0	A
Apr.	4	Aberavon	W	8	0	H
	10	Pontardawe	W	9	0	H
	11	Newport	L	3	9	A
	13	Belfast Collegians	W	12	4	H
	14	Northampton	W	18	3	H
	18	Aberavon	L	0	7	A
	25	Mountain Ash	C	-	-	A
				273	166	

Played	37
Won	21
Drawn	4
Lost	12

Neath RFC, results 1913/14.

Four
Freethy and Juniors

Schoolboy and junior rugby has long flourished in Neath. In the 1880s, the senior club organised the Mills Challenge Cup for local sides, and the cause of development has been taken up by numerous individuals over the years. Prime amongst them must be Albert E. Freethy, whose association with schoolboy rugby started in 1906. Freethy was a schoolteacher at Alderman Davies' School and played full back for the Blacks prior to the First World War. He subsequently went on to captain Neath Cricket Club. His dedicated work with the Neath Schoolboys bore fruit in the production of a number of first-class players and he established a team of 'Ex-Schoolboys' or Neath Wanderers who were virtually invincible. He was also a top-class referee and officiated in 20 internationals as well as the 1924 Olympic Final between France and the USA. Here he is being introduced to the future Edward VIII prior to one of the many Varsity matches that he refereed.

Neath Abbey RFC, *c.* 1900. Neath Abbey were a prominent junior team who produced, among others, Bill Jones. In the 1880s they once played Llanelly and Neath, but went out of existence prior to the First World War.

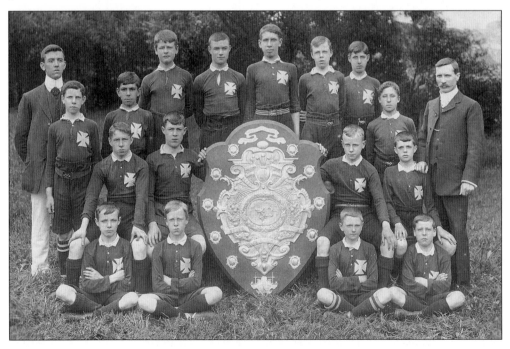

Neath Schoolboys, winners of the Dewar Shield in 1905/06. Included in the line-up are Glyn Stephens, T.A.L. Davies and W.J. Perry, who would all make their marks in senior rugby.

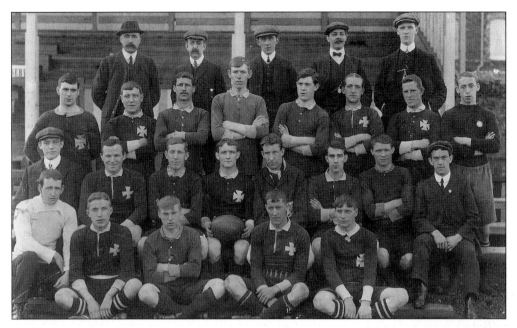

Neath's Second XV emulated the seniors and held a ground record in 1908/09. From left to right, back row: N.R. Phillips, Bert Stephens, W.J. Moon (secretary), R.Vaughan, T.Stephens (chairman). Third row: D. Hoskins, H. Harding, R.T. Rees, D.H. Rees, G. Stephens, E. Thomas, H. Hopes, J. Hughes. Second row: E. Edwards, R.T. Davies, W. Morgan, J. Evans (captain), G. Thomas (vice captain), S. Abraham, E. Evans, H. Davies. Front row: T. Evans (trainer), W. Thomas, W. Parker, J. Thomas, E. Davies.

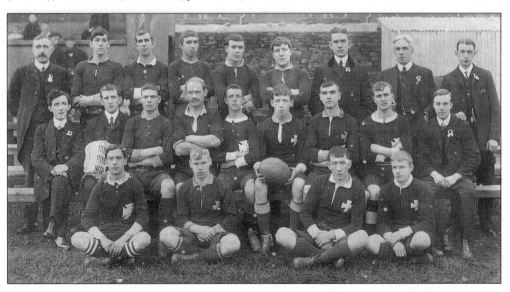

The Neath & District League was formed in 1902 and the following group represented the smaller clubs in the area in 1908/09. From left to right, back row: N.R. Phillips, R. Davies, D. Hughes, D. Wedlake, W. Hill, H. Harding, M. Arnold (chairman), H. Jones, T. Lovering. Middle row: G. Davies, T. Evans (trainer), J. Brown, F. Wooton, W.J. Jones, T. Jones (captain), D. Parry, H. Williams, J.L. Thomas. Front row: D.Evans, W. Parker, W. Thomas, D. Evans.

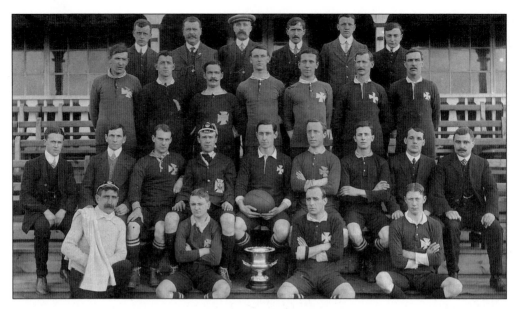

Another popular side was the Neath Crusaders, who played on Thursdays (half-day closing). They became known as the 'Shoppoes' and such sides existed in Swansea, Llanelli and other well populated areas. In 1909/10, Neath Crusaders were champions of the Swansea & District Thursday League. From left to right, back row: C. Heard, R. Jenkins, N.R. Phillips, D. Arnold, E.P. Hemming, W.L. Jones. Third row: W.H. Pyart, W. Davies, S.H. Stacey, W. Hopkins, T. Davies, T Brown, W.L. Jones. Second row: R.D. Rosser (secretary), T.H. Harris (treasurer), V. Taylor, I. Jones, J.H. Moule (captain), T.L. Vaughan, A. Lake, H. Lake (chairman), J. Steer (vice chairman). Front row: W.Bray (trainer), E. Francis, W. Moore, A. James.

Neath Crusaders won the League the following season 1910/11 and added the Edwin Hall Cup for good measure. From left to right, back row: C. Heard, T.H. Harris, D. Arnold, N.R. Phillips, S.H. Stacey, Rees Jenkins. Third row: Sandy Moore (vice chairman), A. Thomas, A. Lake, T. Brown, W.H. Pyart, W. Hopkins, P. Howells, A. Davies, T. Davies, R.D. Rosser (secretary). Second row: V. Taylor, H. Markham, W. Davies (vice captain), J.H. Moule (captain), Edwin Hemming (chairman), J. Morgan, H. Lake, B. Rosser. Front row: T. Lewis, W. Thomas, E. Francis, E. Thomas, W. Moore, A. James, W. Bray (trainer).

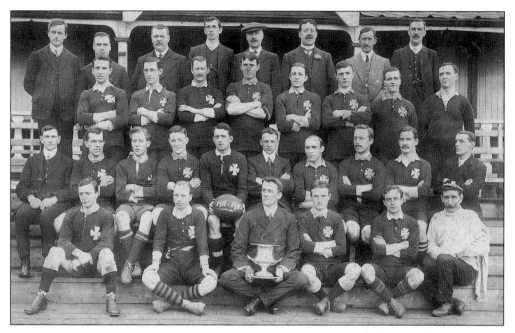

The Swansea & District Thursday League Cup was won again in 1911/12 by Neath Crusaders. From left to right, back row: C. Heard, A. Moore, R. Jenkins, G. Rees, N.R. Phillips, H. Hooper, D. Arnold, E. Watkins. Third row: T.A.L. Davies, J.H. Moule, T. Brown, W. Pyart, W. Moule, J.G. Rees, A. Payne, P. Howells. Second row: T. Harris (treasurer), T. Lewis, A. Hooper, D.J. Stephens, W. Davies (captain), E.P. Hemming (captain), W. Moore, T.L. Vaughan, S.H. Stacey, H. Lake. Front row: Ll. Jones, T.M. Markham, T. Francis (secretary), D. Parker, Theo Davies, W. Bray (trainer).

Neath Crusaders enjoyed an invincible season in 1912/13. From left to right, back row: B. Stevens (trainer), J. Harris, J. Moule, T. Brown (vice captain), T. Davies, A.J. Thomas, J. Green, H. Lake, E. Hemming. Middle row: E.T. Watkins (secretary), B. Evans, B. John, P. Howells (captain), T. Markham, A. Davies, J. Parsons, C. Heard. Front row: S. Stacey, D. Parsons, Ll. Jones, E. Williams.

Neath Quins were another enterprising junior outfit. This Neath Quins party toured France in 1913/14. Alas, they were not the last to leave Neath for France. In the years that immediately followed, many Neath men made the trip to France in service of King and Country … all too many never to return. From left to right, back row: E.D. Williams, D.J. Owen, F. Thomas, G. Hiorns. Third row: V. Williams, S. Webber, T.J. Bowen, A. Jenkins, D.J. Jones. Second row: S. Deakin, W. Harris, T. Bone, J. Jones (captain), S. Williams, T.A. Dryden, J. Evans. Front row: W.H. Roberts, G. Morgan, D. Harry.

The Neath County School kept the rugby tradition going during the war and in 1917/18 they boasted an unbeaten record.

Despite the war, 'muscular Christianity' still held sway amongst those who had survived and amongst those too young to have fought. Pictured in the grounds of St Thomas, Neath are the Neath Church XV. Seated centrally is their president, Rector Gwilym Francis, to his right is captain L.G. Cornwell who played for Neath occasionally, as did the man on his right, H.L. Crabtree.

Neath Schoolboys, 1921/22. From left to right, back row: W.M. Thomas, Haydn Williams, R.T. Williams, Ted Hopkins, T.J. Davies (treasurer), D.W. Prosser, P.L. Griffiths. Third row: Fred Evans (vice chairman), S. Harris, L. Thomas, D. Evans, P. Green, W. Morris, D. Bevan, S. Parker, Sid Harris, Garrett James. Second row: J. Walter Jones (chairman), C. Beynon, S. Bates, W. Evans, L. Shipton, E.H. Jones (captain), N. Jenkins, T. Day, G. Bridgeman, B. Sandham, A.E. Freethy (secretary). Front row: S. Hickman, T. Davies, W. Griffiths.

Neath Schoolboys produced four internationals in 1921/22. This group includes Len Shipton, Tom Day, Albert Freethy (secretary), Howie Jones and Noel Jenkins.

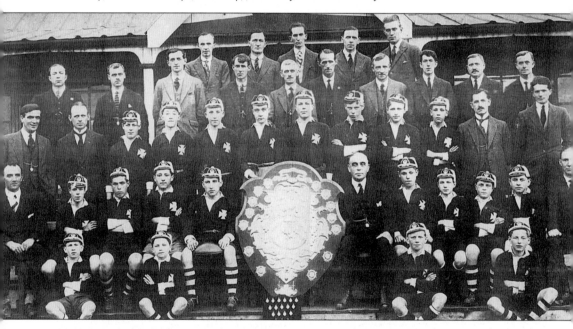

In 1922/23, Neath Schoolboys won all 19 games, scoring 385 points with just 39 against. They brought back the Dewar Shield to Neath. From left to right, top: Messrs E. Hopkins, W.M. Thomas, L. Powell, J.H. Williams, Les Smith. Back row: Messrs. W.J. Cole, D.J. Thomas, Geo. Rees, T. Cole, Fred Richards, T.J. Thomas, G.F. Lloyd, E. Burrows, P. Burrows, J. Burrows. Third row: Mr J. Oaks, Mr D.W. Prosser, M. Lewis, C. Griffiths, R. Williams, I. Quick, I. Bevan, I. Rees, S. Harris, T. Parker, Mr T.G. James, Mr T.J. Davies (treasurer). Second row: A.E. Freethy (secretary), F. Tyler, C. Beynon, G. Bevan, S. Bates (captain), Capt. W.E. Rees JP (president), B. Sandham, T. Walters, I. Herbert, A. Reed, J. Walter Jones (chairman). Front row: O. Greenwood, E. Rees, T. Davies, W. Griffiths.

Neath Schoolboys held the remarkable record of being invincible in 1922/23, 1923/24 and 1924/25. Their success led to Freethy forming his 'Ex-Schoolboys XV' or 'Neath Wanderers', as they became known. They played at Court Herbert (Neath Athletic's home today) and drew crowds comparable with Neath. Many of the team played for Neath, several for Swansea, including the internationals Howie Jones and Tom Day. From left to right, back row: Messrs. W.J. Cole, D.R. Edwards, C. Heard, Jno. Bowen, T.G. Grandfield (treasurer), Jno. Williams, T. Cole, Alf Thomas, D. Davies. Third row: R. Williams, C. Harris, T. Parker, T. Day, W. Morris, P. Green, I. Bevan, I. Quick, I. Rees, F. Tyler. Second row: Mr A.E. Freethy (secretary), C. Beynon, S. Bates, P. Steer, G. Bevan, E.H. Jones (captain), D. Rees, S. Harris, W. Evans, A. Reed, Mr Willie Hopkins (chairman). Front row: T. Davies, T. Walters, W. Thomas, J. Peat.

Neath Schools won the Dewar Shield in 1924/25. Seated third left is D.M. Evans who went on to play for Neath and figured in a Welsh final trial ten years later. In front (left) is Gwyn Moore, rated the finest centre ever to play for Neath.

Freethy's most (in)famous hour. Never before had a referee sent a player from an international field. Freethy made history in 1925 when he gave New Zealand's Cyril Brownlie his marching orders – and in front of King George V too!

MAGNIFICENT TRIUMPH ATTENDED BY TRAGEDY.

By "OBSERVER."

	G.	T.	Pts.
New Zealand	*2	3	17
England	*2	1	11

*One penalty.

New Zealand's tour of England, Ireland, and Wales ended in a triumph and a tragedy—triumph because they won their twenty-eighth consecutive victory, and tragedy because one of their players was sent from the field in the early stages for rough play. Cyril Brownlie was the central figure in this match, and for many years to come the "Brownlie incident" will be constantly cropping up wherever Rugby people gather.

Was Brownlie the culprit? Did such drastic punishment fit the offence? Was the referee justified in taking such extreme measures in an international match—and before Royalty, too? These questions will be asked, and answered with as little chance of unanimity as that concerning Dean's "try" in 1905.

Mr. A. E. Freethy, of Neath, was the referee, and throughout the world of Rugby he is known as a fearless official. Those who know him will at once appreciate the fact that when he gave the big Brownlie marching orders he was fully alive to the storm of criticism which would arise. That the happening did much to tone down the unruly element in the game was apparent from subsequent play.

Mr. Freethy alleges that Brownlie kicked an opponent, and no sportsman will question the fact that the only course open to the official when such an offence is committed is to send the offender from the field of play.

When the game started most of us sensed the feelings of some of the players, and were not unprepared for a display of the bad feeling which has a nasty habit of being introduced into some of our Rugby games when there is something big at stake. The prize for New Zealand was to complete a tour of this country with an unbroken list of victories, and for England to break the sequence. Since Rugby has been taken up by the home countries, international game referees have shown a marked dislike to meeting displays of temper with the extreme penalty which they would at once impose in club games. At Swansea last year there were cases of sheer brutality which well merited a couple of men being ordered to the

THE BROWNLIE INCIDENT.

MR. FREETHY GIVES HIS VERSION.

Among the New Zealand players the impression was that had Mr. Freethy sent off an Englishman with Cyril Brownlie they would have thought his action more just. They state that he is the most able referee who has controlled their games, but think he made a mistake when he singled out Brownlie. They look upon the latter as the scapegoat for a number of "incidents" in which Englishmen were well to the fore.

Mr. Freethy is equally certain that he picked out the offender, and after the game remarked :—

"Without mincing any words, I say that Brownlie walked right away from the ball and deliberately kicked a man who was lying on the ground.

"I have admired Brownlie's play for a long time, but the conclusion I have come to after this afternoon's match is that he is too apt to lose his temper. Before the match I spoke with all the good will in the world to both the captains, and emphasised that they should impress on their players to keep their temper.

"I had warned two players on either side and had given two general warnings to the teams before I ordered Brownlie off the field. It hurt me very much to take this action, but what Brownlie did was so deliberate that I am afraid I was tempted to watch him at the moment rather than watch the play. After what I saw I had not the slightest hesitation in taking the action I did."

Brownlie gave a total denial to the charge of kicking, and added :—

"It was a piece of sheer bad luck on my part. I found myself involved in a series of minor retaliations, and I was unfortunate enough to be dropped on.

"I am very sorry the thing has happened in this last match of a splendid season. Although I feel very sore about it, there is no ill feeling over the matter.

"I absolutely deny the referee's allegation that I kicked a man on the ground."

Mr. S. S. Dean, the manager of the New Zealand team, said :—

"After hearing the statement of the referee we are of the opinion that in this particular instance he has made a mistake. I have spoken to all our players, and they are unanimously agreed that no such action as is alleged was committed."

Most newspaper reports considered that Freethy was fully justified in taking this ultimate sanction and, if anything, his reputation was enhanced by his brave action.

The Prince of Wales saw New Zealand beat England on Saturday at Twickenham by a goal from a try, a penalty goal, and three tries, to a goal from a try, a penalty goal, and a try – 17 points to 11. The Prince received a rousing reception from the record crowd – there were some 60,000 persons on the ground.

Unfortunately the opening of this really great match was marred by unusual and excessive unpleasantness. Scrapping in the scrummage began immediately, and in a minute or two blows were struck. Twice did Mr Freethy, the referee, warn an Englishman, and twice did he warn a New Zealander. His warnings having apparently no effect, he blew his whistle and told both sets of forwards that on the next occasion he would send the offender off the field. The next occasion came all too quickly, when the game was only ten minutes old.

Mr Freethy said that he saw Cyril Brownlie 'deliberately kick a player lying on the ground', and he ordered him off the field in consequence. Mr Freethy had issued his warnings, and he had to be as good as his word. Never before have I seen such action taken in an international match, and in justice to the punished player, I ought to say that he had a reputation of being a very fair one. Mr Freethy refereed magnificently, and in less capable hands than his this game would have become just chaos.

Freethy is presented to King George V at a Twickenham international.

Albert Freethy in his characteristic striped blazer pictured with the Irish XV prior to their 4-3 win over England at Lansdowne Road, Dublin on 8 February 1930.

Five
Back from the Front

Glyn Stephens was a key member of the Neath and Wales pack before the First World War. He became the first Neath player to captain his country when he led Wales against the New Zealand Army XV in 1919. Unfortunately, that was his record tenth and final appearance for his country because a neck injury forced Stephens to retire. His retirement certainly set back Neath's plans for reconstruction after the war. Stephens concentrated on his local mining interests and was soon elected to the Neath Committee and later to the WRU. He became president of the WRU in 1956/57 and his son Rees followed in his footsteps, captaining Neath and Wales during an international career which spanned a then record 32 caps.

Neath Football Club & Athletic Association.

NEATH,

May, 1915.

DEAR SIR,

AT an Extraordinary General Meeting of Members of this Club, held at the Town Hall, on Tuesday, the 20th inst., the financial position of the Association was placed before the members which showed that at the present moment the Club's liabilities amount to £487 : 7 : 8, and a resolution was carried that the members and friends of the Association should be appealed to for financial support with a view of keeping the Association going.

The Trustees of the Gnoll Estate have met the Association very liberally by foregoing 12 months' rent of the field, from September, 1914, to September, 1915, and our Secretary has voluntary decided to forego his 12 months' salary, £50. The Committee earnestly hope that the spirit displayed by the Trustees of the Gnoll Estate and our esteemed Secretary, is the spirit in which the appeal we are now making will be met by the members of the Club and our friends generally.

We have at the present moment 14 of our playing members serving with the Colours, which number includes our Captain who has been in France from the outbreak of War, and having abandoned all our matches, we respectfully ask you to kindly help us to keep the Association afloat by continuing your Annual Subscription and by subscribing to the funds as liberally as you can, so that when our playing members return they will find that we at home have done our share to keep the Club going.

We therefore await with confidence your early and favourable reply.

On behalf of the Committee,

> **J. E. MOORE-GWYN, President,**
> **MATTHEW ARNOLD, Mayor of Neath,**
> **C. POWELL, Chairman of Committee,**
> **JONAH ARNOLD, Hon. Treasurer,**
> **ARTHUR L. DAVID, Secretary.**

The subject of the club debt occupied many an AGM in the pre-war era and this document represents an appeal for help from the committee to keep rugby alive during the harsh wartime years.

Neath's first Barbarian was full-back J.L.G. Thomas. 'Doctor Gwyn' as he was known played his first game before the war.

A public meeting was held to re-launch the club after the war.

Feb.	22	Skewen	W	6	0	H
Mar.	1	Glyncorrwg	W	7	0	H
	8	38th Welsh Division	L	3	15	H
	15	Pontardawe	W	17	3	H
	22	Llanelly	W	8	0	H
	29	Swansea	L	3	15	A
Apr.	5	Pontrhydyfen	W	25	0	H
	12	Llwynypia	C	-	-	A
	18	Mr. Harry David's XV	W	16	5	H
	19	New Zealand Army	L	3	10	H
	21	WALES 3 pts NEW ZEALAND ARMY XV 6 pts (at Swansea)				
	21	R.A.F.	L	3	8	H
	22	Swansea	W	4	0	H
	26	Skewen	L	0	4	A
	29	Llanelly	L	0	15	A
				95	75	
		Played	13			
		Won	7			
		Drawn	0			
		Lost	6			

Neath's first 'season' after the war was limited to just 13 games.

Glyn Gethin was the first Neath back since Sam Clarke to be capped by Wales in their Paris victory of 1913. Gethin led the Blacks in their truncated 1918/19 season and probably had a few years of top class rugby left in him but he made way at full-back for the up and coming J.L.G. Thomas.

One of England's all-time greats W.W. Wakefield (later Lord Kendal) married a Neath girl and turned out for the Blacks during vacations.

Neath played the New Zealand Army XV without Glyn Stephens, who was rested for the international.

ROUGH PLAY AT NEATH.

SEVERAL CASUALTIES IN MATCH WITH NEW ZEALAND.

	G.	T.	Pts.
NEW ZEALAND	2	0	10
NEATH	0	1	3

Neath were at home to a New Zealand XV. There was a large crowd present. The teams were:—

NEATH.—Back, Glyn Gethin; three-quarter backs, W. Millett, Vernon Hill, Bryn Davies, and Oswald Williams; half-backs, Con Evans and C. Heard; forwards, P.C. Perry, P.C. Will Hopkins, P.C. Jenkin Hopkins, Jack Jones, Bob Randall, D. Edwards, W. Powell, and Ivor Evans.

NEW ZEALAND.—Back, H Capper; three-quarter backs, E. Ryan, B. Roberts, and G. Owles; five-eights, C. Grey and McGibbon; half-back, B. Sandman; forwards, Lucas, Sellars, Stindon, Lockbrune, Gilchrist, Douglas, Allan, and Tapene.

Referee: Capt. Bird (Cardiff).

Neath for a short time had to play fourteen men, Vernon Hill not having arrived. The home side kicked off and faced the sun. After a smart movement Lucas scored for the visitors behind the posts, Capper converting.

Again the Colonials pressed, and Richards made a splendid run for the line, but his pass was forward. Neath were now doing much better, but they were unable to get beyond the centre line. Then came a splendid run by Allan, who was tackled within a few yards of the line, and from the ensuing play Hill brought much needed relief, which, however, gave Neath only a moment's respite, for a long kick gained touch well over the 25 line. The Colonials kept up the pressure, and Neath twice touched down behind the line.

There was an exciting moment, a series of scrums being fought on the Colonial line.

Then Lucas was penalised. Powell took the kick and piloted the ball over the bar amidst tremendous enthusiasm.

Resuming, Neath had the advantage of a slight breeze and the sun behind them. It was estimated that by the interval there were 8,000 spectators present. From the centre-line Jenkins made an opening for Hill, but the latter knocked on. From the scrum Hill received and passed to Millett. The latter sprinted to the line and punted over Capper's head. There was an exciting chase for possession, and the Colonial just got there in time to kick the ball out of play. After this incident Lucas was seen lying on the ground apparently winded, and the crowd became impatient. The Colonials were penalised, but Capper replied with a strong run to the centre.

Play on the resumption was dangerously rough, and several home players were injured, but kept going. Con Evans was injured on the knee, and Williams had a limp.

Play fluctuated until Gilchrist picked up in the loose and got over on his own behind the post. Capper converted.

Wakefield captained England to the Grand Slam in 1925. Here he is pictured with his team prior to the international that season at Swansea.

DATE 1920	FIRST TEAM MATCHES, 1920-21 OPPONENTS	Ground	Result	NEATH G	T	P	OPPONENT G	T	P
Sept. 4	District League	Home							
,, 11	Ammanford	Home							
,, 18	Pontardawe	Home							
,, 25	Maesteg	Home							
Oct. 2	Llanelly	Away							
,, 9	Northampton	Away							
,, 11	Bedford { Tour	Away							
,, 16	Cardiff	Home							
,, 23	Cross Keys	Away							
,, 30	Swansea	Home							
Nov. 6	Aberavon	Away							
,, 13	Mountain Ash	Home							
,, 18	W.F.U. West. Trial M.	Home							
,, 20	Maesteg	Away							
,, 25	Newport (Thursday)	Away							
,, 27	Llanelly	Home							
Dec. 4	Aberavon	Home							
,, 11	Swansea	Away							
,, 18	Pontypridd	Home							
,, 25	London Welsh (Xmas)	Home							
,, 27	London Irish (B.D.)	Home							
,, 28	Swansea (Tuesday)	Away							
1921 Jan. 1	Llanelly	Away							
,, 8	Aberavon	Away							
,, 15	Swansea	Home							
,, 22	Bridgend	Home							
,, 29	Pontardawe	Away							
Feb. 5	Scotland v. Wales	Sw's'a							
,, 12	Pontypool	Home							
,, 19	Mountain Ash	Away							
,, 26	Llanelly	Home							
March 5	Briton Ferry	Away							
,, 7	Pontypridd (Monday)	Away							
,, 12	Swansea	Away							
,, 19	Aberavon	Home							
,, 25	Briton Ferry (G. Fri.)	Home							
,, 26	Northampton	Home							
,, 28	Headingly (E. Monday)	Home							
,, 29	Cross Keys (E. Tuesday)	Home							
April 2	Devonport United Serv.	Home							
,, 9	Newport	Home							
,, 16	Pontypool	Away							
,, 23	Bridgend	Away							
,, 30	Cardiff	Away							

1920/21 season ticket and fixtures.

Will Hopkins, a local police officer, led Neath in 1919/20 which was only moderately successful as they ended with 20 wins, 2 draws and 19 defeats. From left to right, back row: T.Davies (trainer), F.W. David, J.B. Williams, A.E. Freethy, C. Williams, C. Heard, A.W.M. Tench (treasurer), G. Hopes, W. Gabriel, P. Howells. Third row: D.H. Davies, Rev. A.T. Lewis, A. Hopkins, D. Vigors, Tal Davies, W.J. Perry, A. Baker, J. Jones, Bert Thomas, G. Watkins, M. Lloyd, A.L. David (secretary). Second row: D.R. Edwards, T. Davies, Ernie Thomas, W. Hill, W.H. Evans, W. Hopkins (captain), W. Millett, B. Richards, W.L. Loveluck, L. Edwards, J. Morris, W.B. Morgan. Front row: W.E. Allin, P. Hughes, A. Morgan, S. Evans.

Neath played the Barbarians three times immediately after the First World War, winning twice and drawing once. The games were played on Easter Tuesday and drew great crowds to the Gnoll. Fixtures ceased allegedly because Neath's Will Powell leapt high to divert a Ba-Ba's kick at goal in 1922 – an action which was considered unsporting by the famous club who did not revisit Neath until 1971/72 during Neath's centenary.

Neath versus Barbarians

1921
Mar. 29. Lost to Neath, 2 goals (10 pts.) to 1 penalty goal, 3 tries (12 pts.).
BARBARIANS—D. M. Houston; A. M. M'Gregor, A. M. David, P. K. Albertijn, C. L. Steyn; A. T. Young, J. C. Seager; H. L. G. Hughes (captain), E. F. Turner, F. H. X. Gwynne, D. D. Morton, F. le S. Stone, V. Grenning, R. S. Hellier, W. J. Jenkins.
Scorers—Try each by David and Steyn (both converted by Steyn).
NEATH—L. G. Thomas (captain); D. Harris, Glyn Morgan, E. Evans, R. V. Hill; L. Phillips, T. O. Francis; D. D. Hiddlestone, A. Baker, W. E. Thomas, G. Watkins, A. Hopkins, J. Thomas, C. Bannister, W. Powell.
Scorers—Try each by W. E. Thomas, Evans and Hopkins. Penalty goal by Powell.
Referee—J. Thomas (Swansea).

1923
Apr. 3. Lost to Neath, 1 goal (5 pts.) to 1 dropped goal, 4 tries (16 pts.).
BARBARIANS — D. Drysdale; D. R. Wheeler, J. C. Seager, G. G. Aitken, J. L. F. Steele; I. D. Bowen, J. R. Wheeler; M. P. Atkinson (captain), D. Marsden-Jones, L. W. Haslett, F. Spriggs, H. N. Knox, J. D. Clinch, C. F. G. T. Hallaran, A. E. Beith.
Scorers—Try by Bowen, converted by Drysdale.
NEATH—Ivor Jones; S. Jenkins, W. Smith, J. G. Jones, L. Stoddart; B. Peters, T. H. Francis; A. Baker, D. D. Hiddlestone, J. John, F. Coope, Moses Davies, S. Daymond, L. Edwards, W. Gleaves.
Scorers—Tries by Smith (2), Jenkins and Coope. Dropped goal by Francis.

1924
Apr. 22. Drew with Neath, each side scoring 1 goal, 2 tries (11 pts.)
BARBARIANS—W. E. Crawford; I. S. Smith, R. L. Raymond, G. G. Aitken (captain), Rowe Harding; E. J. Massey, A. C. Wallace; J. C. R. Buchanan, I. M. B. Stuart, W. E. Tucker, H. L. G. Hughes, D. Marsden-Jones, E. R. Barrett, A. E. Beith, A. F. Blakiston.
Scorers—Try each by Harding (converted by Crawford), Smith and Wallace
NEATH—Ivor Jones; D. Harris, J. G. Jones, W. R. Smith, G. Phillips; E. Watkins, E. Williams; D. D. Hiddlestone, W. Perry, I. Thomas, S. Daymond, D. Phillips, D. R. Jenkins, T. Davies, P. Jones.
Scorers—Tries by Parry, G. Phillips (converted by Thomas) and Watkins.
Referee—R. Fearn (Mountain Ash).

Neath RFC, 1920/21. Neath's recovery from the war was slow, if steady, and they ended with a record of Played 43, Won 21, Drawn 5, Lost 17, Points For 307, Points Against 257. J.L.G. Thomas captained Neath in 1920/21. Seated third from the left is Eric Evans, a wing three-quarter for Neath, who succeeded Walter E. Rees as secretary of the WRU in 1948 until 1955.

Forward Ambrose Baker was the first Neath player to be newly capped after the war. He is pictured (back row, third from right) in the combined England-Wales XV which played Scotland-Ireland to mark the centenary of Rugby School. After winning 5 caps, Baker joined Oldham RL and was a big loss to Neath as they sought to discover pre-war glories.

Neath's second Barbarian was R. Vernon Hill. He captained Neath in 1921/22.

Neath RFC, 1922/23. Jack Jones' side Played 41 Won 20 Drawn 2 Lost 19, Points For 346 Points Against 262. From left to right, back row: T.Phillips (trainer), J. John, P. Howells, S. Daymond, A.W.M. Tench (treasurer), P. Jones, A.E. Freethy, W. Gleaves, J. Williams, C. Heard. Third row: A.L. David (secretary), B. Sutcliffe (treasurer), L. Edwards, F. Coope, A. Baker, E. Harris, Jack Thomas, Dan Davies, W. Jones. Second row: Rev. G. Francis, W.B. Morgan, D. Hiddlestone, J.G. Jones, W.R. Smith, Jack Jones (captain), E. Watkins, W.E. Allin, I. Jones, S. Evans (trainer). Front row: P. Mellin, S. Jenkins, T.H. Francis, B. Peters.

W.J. Davies joined Neath from Resolven in 1922, but this classy centre soon departed for Castleford RLFC, where he gained Wales international honours.

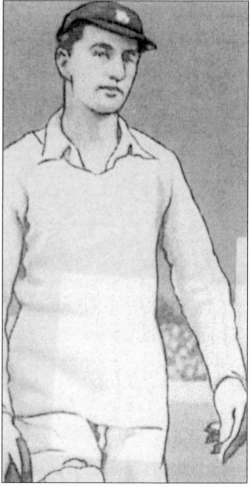

W.J. Davies was sometimes partnered by C.F. (Cyril) Walters, who is best known for his cricketing exploits with Worcestershire and England. Walters was no mean rugby player either and turned out for Neath and later Swansea.

Neath RFC, 1923/24. The Blacks produced their best yet post-war season under the captaincy of Ivor Jones. Their record read: Played 46, Won 29, Drawn 4, Lost 13. From left to right, back row: C. Heard, J. John, T. Davies, L. Edwards, M. Davies, M. Cole, A.W.M. Tench (treasurer), A.L. David (secretary). Third row: P. Howells, D.R. Edwards, I. Thomas, W.J. Perry, P. Jones, S. Daymond, D. Jenkins, D. Phillips, Sgt W. Hopkins, F.W. David. Second row: Shon Evans (trainer), W.B. Jones, D. Harris, J.G. Jones, D. Hiddlestone, I. Jones (captain), W.B. Morgan (chairman), W.R. Smith, G. Phillips, A.E. Freethy, A.J. Mills. Front row: S. Jenkins, E. Williams, E. Watkins, C. Heard junior, Theo Davies.

An appeal for funds was made to members as Neath sought to improve facilities at The Gnoll.

Neath Football Club & Athletic Association.

President   -   -   -   Capt. W. E. REES, J.P.

CAEGROES TERRACE,
CADOXTON,
NEAR NEATH,
19th July, 1923.

Dear Sir,

The Committee of the above Club have been discussing the ways and means of erecting a Club House on the Ground, in consequence of the very unsatisfactory accommodation now available under the Grand Stand, and which is quite inadequate for the needs of the Players, and not in keeping with the status of the Neath Club.

The Committee have leased from the Neath Corporation, for a term of 70 years, a portion of the Allotment Ground adjoining the Football Field, where it is intended to erect the Club House. The cost of such building has been estimated at £1,300.

Having regard to the present financial position of the Club, it is felt that the funds of the Club will not justify the expenditure of this amount, but a suggestion has been made that an appeal should be made to the members to subscribe by way of a loan an amount of say 10/- and upwards, free of interest, to enable the Club to proceed immediately with the erection of the building. Arrangements will be made to refund a certain amount annually (as the finances of the Club will permit) to the Subscribers in liquidation of the debt.

The Committee confidently appeal for your kind consideration and financial support, and I shall be pleased to receive the attached form duly completed at your earliest convenience.

Yours faithfully,

ARTHUR L. DAVID,
Secretary.

NEATH FOOTBALL CLUB.

PROPOSED NEW CLUB HOUSE.

I shall be pleased to subscribe by way of a loan, free of interest, the sum of £   :   :   , towards the fund being raised for payment of the above Club House.

Name ....

Address ....

Scrum-half D.M.Davies joined Neath from Amman United, but was quickly snapped up by Broughton Rangers R.L. He also appeared in four RL Challenge Cup finals, but had the misfortune to finish on the losing side each time. As this programme shows, D.M. appeared in the Wales XIII which defeated England 10-4 in 1930.

Neath RFC, 1924/25. Dai Hiddlestone led Neath to a record of Played 38, Won 21, Drawn 4, Lost 13. Hiddlestone was another forceful character in the true Neath mould. When playing for Wales against New Zealand, he led the Welsh team in an impromptu war-dance in response to the Kiwi 'haka'. He later took up the whistle – a 'poacher turned game-keeper' if ever there was! From left to right, back row: C. Heard, A.L. David (secretary), W.B. Jones, D.H. Davies, F.W. David, Sgt W. Hopkins, A.J. Mills. Third row: J. Morris, G. Edwards, D. Pascoe, S. Daymond, M. Cole, P. Jones, D.R. Jenkins, T. Evans, M. Davies, D. Phillips, T. Arthur. Second row: D.R. Edwards, A.E. Freethy, W.J. Davies, T. Bevan, G. Phillips, P. Howells (chairman), D. Hiddlestone (captain), I. Jones, I. Davies, G. Morgan, H. Thomas, T. Davies, W.B. Morgan. Front row: E. Williams, D.M. Davies.

Six
Champions Again!

Tom Evans joined Neath in 1924/25 from Amman United and soon established himself as a regular in the Neath pack which was slowly regaining its fearsome pre-war reputation. In a pack of truly great forwards, Tom Evans was a real leader. He captained Neath in 1928/29 when they won their first inter-war championship and his team might well have repeated the feat in 1929/30. However, Tom Evans 'had his leg broken' in a win at Resolven in March 1930 and the side fell away to lose 6 out of their last 10 games without him and missed out on a back-to-back championship title.

Neath were steadily rebuilding the side when long-serving forward Jim John led them in 1925/26 when their record read: Played 41, Won 21, Drew 2, Lost 18 with 517 points for, 386 against. From left to right, back row: F.W. David, H. Davies, D. Pascoe, T. Evans, G. Edwards, T. Arthur, G. Hopkins, D.H. Davies, G. Callard. Third row: A.L. David (secretary), P.G. Jenkins, E. Harris, E. Gethin, W. Gleaves, T. Vaughan, S. Daymond, G. Barclay, Alderman J. Cook Rees, P. Howells. Second row: S. Evans (trainer), W.B. Morgan, D. Jones, W.J. Davies, J. John (captain), T. Davies (chairman), T. Bowen, I. Thomas, J. Morris, A.J. Mills. Front row: J. Owen, T. Bevan.

Former Bridgend and Wales forward Dan Pascoe, an accurate goal-kicker, became captain in 1926/27 before going north and handing over to wing Dan Jones.

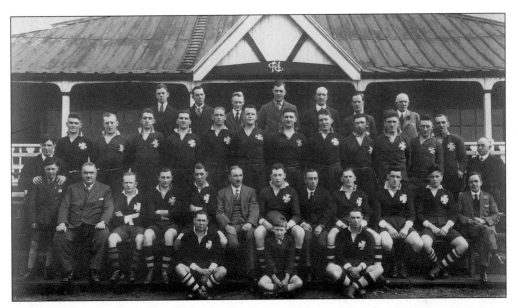

Welsh trialist forward George Edwards was captain in 1927/28 when Neath enjoyed a very successful year. Their record – Played 47, Won 33, Drawn 3, Lost 11, Points For 602, Points Against 203 – very nearly brought them the championship. From left to right, top: R.T. Richards, W.G. Price, G. Callard, G. Stephens, E.J. Thomas, P.G. Jenkins, Coun. W. Waring. Back row: S. Evans (trainer), H. Davies, G. Barclay, A. Lemon, D. Evans, T. Evans, E. Martin, T. Arthur, G. Hopkins, A. Davies, E. Bowen, R.H. Garbett, T. Hollingdale, J. Morris. Middle row: Supt. Rees Davies, S. Rees, E. Jones, D. Jones, A.J. Mills (vice chairman), G. Edwards (captain), Archie J. Morris (Secretary & Treasurer), G. Daniels, P. Lloyd, A. Hickman, T. Davies. Front row: E. Matthews, R. Davies junior, J. Owen.

Neath forward Tom Hollingdale, in predatory mood, about to pounce on an Irishman in Wales' 10-13 defeat at Cardiff in March 1928. Tom Hollingdale, capped 6 times, was from the traditional hard school of Neath forwards and, on retirement, he took up the cloth and became a clergyman in London.

Neath RFC, 1928/29 – Welsh Champions. Played 49, Won 42, Drawn 3, Lost 4, Points For 930 (World Record), Points Against 230. Inset: Dan Jones, Howie Jones. From left to right, back row: W.G. Price, Coun. H. Waring, Chief Const. P.D. Keep, A. Davies, A. Lemon, D. Evans, G. Hopkins, T. Arthur, W.H. Waring, J. Dummer, E.J. Thomas. Third row: R.T. Davies (assistant secretary), G. Stephens, H. Davies, T. Hollingdale, E. Bowen, C. Pugh, Harold Jones, T.H. Morgan, H. Thomas, G. Barclay, G. Callard, S. Evans (trainer). Second row: Rev. G. Francis MA, Supt R. Davies, P. Lloyd, E. Jones, A.J. Mills (chairman), T. Evans (captain), A.J. Morris (secretary and treasurer), I. Thomas, A. Hickman, T. Davies, R. Williams. Front row: J. Owen, G. Daniels, H. Rees.

Another team group from 1928/29.

Captain : Tom Evans ; Vice-Captain : Emrys Jones.

Unofficial Welsh Champions.

Record : **Played 49, Won 42, Drawn 3, Lost, 4, Points for 930, Against, 232.**

The points scored is]a record for any Welsh Club.

The detailed record reads :

Opponents.	Points.		Opponents.	Points	
Sept., 1928.			**Feb.**		
1—District League (h)	29	3	9—Ebbw Vale (h)	38	0
8—Resolven (h)	18	0	23—Llanelly (h)	26	6
15—Pontypridd (h)	25	0	28—Bridgend (h)	13	3
22—Newport (a)	3	3	**March.**		
29—Cross Keys (h)	21	3	2—Resolven (a)	11	3
October.			4—Aberavon (a)	0	0
6—Llanelly (a)	8	6	9—Swansea (a)	3	0
13—Aberavon (a)	14	8	16—Aberavon (h)	5	9
21—Swansea (h)	6	4	23—Ebbw Vale (a)	16	3
25—County Police (h)	12	5	28—Swansea (a)	5	21
27—Penarth (h)	28	6	30—Edgware (h)	35	3
November.			**April.**		
3—Cross Keys (h)	5	13	1—Glam. Wand'rs (h)	37	5
10—Edgeware (a)	21	5	2—Abertillery (h)	37	3
12—Brighton	28	3	6—Maesteg (a)	15	8
17—Maesteg (h)	32	4	10—Penarth (a)	11	6
24—Llanelly (h)	29	0	13—Newport (h)	13	0
December.			16—Burton (a)	23	9
1—Aberavon)h)	33	3	17—Derby (a)	19	6
8—Pontypool (h)	26	0	20—Pontypool (a)	25	3
15—Welsh Varsities (h)	32	13	25—Neath Police (h)	31	17
22—Cardiff (a)	9	8	27—Pontypridd (a)	21	3
24—Abertillery (h)	3	0	29—Abertillery (a)	16	3
25—London Welsh (h)	16	3	**May.**		
26—Western Counties (h)	33	0	2—Cwmavon (h)	17	10
Jan, 1929.			4—Cardiff (a)	8	9
12—Llanelly (a)	9	9	6—Briton Ferry (a)	34	0
19—Cardiff (h)	17	3			
26—Bridgend (a)	14	0		**930**	**232**

Dan Jones scored 59 tries (73 in all matches during season). Emrys Jones converted 83 tries, kicked 18 penalty goals, 5 dropped goals, and scored seven tries—a total of 261 points.

Howie Jones scored six tries in one match, against Aberavon at Neath on December 1st, 1929.

The other scorers were : Howie Jones, 21, Glyn Daniels, 20, Hector Davies, 20, A. Hickman, 19, Jim Owen, 14, A. Lemon, 8, Dai Evans, Albert Davies, George Barclay, George Vaughan, J. B. Reynolds, Tom Arthur, 5 each, Harold Jones, Harry Rees, 3 each. Tom Evans, Gordon Hopkins, Willie Evans, Abraham Thomas, Ivor Thomas, 2 each. E. Bowen, Rees Evans, Arthur Davies and T. Morgan 1 each. Barclay 8 con. goals, 3 pen. goals ; Daniels, 2 con. goals, Harry Rees 1 dropped goal. Tom Arthur, A. Lemon and Harold Jones represented Wales during the season.

Committee, Mr. A. J. Mills, chairman, Rev. Gwilym Francis, M.A. vice-chairman, Messrs. D. H. Davies, Theo. Davies, J. Dummer, Phil Howells, P. G. Jenkins, Councillor J. Morris, Lyn Owen, W. G. Price, Ernie Thomas, W. H. Waring, Councillor Herbert Waring and R. C. Williams. Treasurer & Secretary : Mr. Archie J. Morris, M.B.E.

Neath's championship-winning results from 1928/29 as published by a local contemporary.

Neath RFC, 1929/30. Their record: Played 47, Won 32, Drawn 2, Lost 13, Points For 649, Points Against 215 would have been so much better with Tom Evans there to the end. From left to right, back row: P. Howells (vice chairman), W.H. Waring, P.D. Keep, G. Callard, R.C. Williams. Fourth row: R. Gregory, W.G. Price, H.M. Fuller (referee), D.H. Davies, E.J. Thomas, G.H. Mills, L. Owen, J. Dummer. Third row: T. Arthur, D. Evans, A.C. Walsh, T. Parker, G. Hopkins, G. Williams, Rev. G.A.L. Evans, T. Hollingdale, G. Roberts, A. Lemon, A. Davies, T.H. Morgan, E. Price, A.J.Mills. Second row: S. Evans (trainer), Supt R. Davies, E. Davies, G. Bevan, E. Jones, Rev. G. Francis MA, T. Evans (captain), E.R. Whittington-Moe (president), G. Daniel, D. Jones, C.R. Whittington-Moe, A.J. Morris (secretary and treasurer), T. Davies. Front row: J. Owen, S. Evans junior, G. Thomas, R. Davies junior, A. Hickman, J.D. Phillips, G. Moore.

Arthur Lemon, another granite-hewn Neath forward, was capped 13 times for Wales. Unfortunately, like so many Neath men, Lemon joined the exodus north at St Helen's.

Welsh international Tom Hollingdale led Neath in 1930/31. The record read: Played 41, Won 27, Drew 1, Lost 13 with 452 points scored and 248 against. From left to right, back row: W.G. Price, R. Gregory, W.H. Cooper, T. Williams, G.H. Mills, E.J. Thomas, P.D. Keep, J. Shufflebotham, H. Waring, J. Dummer, W.A. Griffiths (assistant secretary), C. Heard. Third row: S. Evans (trainer), G. Moore, T.H. Morgan, G. Prosser, R. Jones, G. Roberts, G. Hopkins, T. Arthur, Rev. G.A.L. Evans, E. Davies, A. Davies, M. Abraham, A.J. Mills. Second row: T. Davies, D. Jones, G. Bevan, G. Daniels, A.J. Morris (secretary and treasurer), T. Hollingdale (captain), P. Howells, G. Thomas, A. Hickman, P. Lloyd, G. Callard. Front row: J. Owen, J.D. Phillips, W. Griffiths, W. Owen.

During the championship-winning season of 1928/29, Neath ran up many big victories no matter what the ground conditions or the opposition were like. In successive weeks in early December they racked up big wins over Aberavon and Pontypool.

NEATH RUN RIOT AT THE GNOLL.

Home Backs in Brilliant Form.

ABERAVON'S DEFENCE RIDDLED.

(By " RECORDER.")

The All Blacks, on Saturday, again proved their claim to be the best team in the Principality. They beat Aberavon by 33 points to three. The Neath pack overwhelmed the visiting octette, both in the open and in the scrummages, and no one did better in every phase of forward play than the newcomer to the side, Harold Jones, the ex-Bridgend forward. Unfortunately, the All Blacks already have a galaxy of splendid forwards, but on Saturday's form a regular place will have to be found for Jones.

The handling of the All Blacks' quartette was faultless, and each man did his part to perfection. Howie Jones was, if one may individualise, the best of the line. Vaughan lacked speed when opposed to Morgan, and had Dan Jones been available, Neath's score might have reached the half-century. Owen and Reynolds again displayed perfect understanding, and were vastly superior to Selby and Thomas. Phil Lloyd was as safe as the proverbial "house," but he had no strong opponent in T. James, who took the place of his namesake, who was engaged in the " trial." The scorers for Neath were Howie Jones (2), Hector Davies (2), Owen, Lemon, and Reynolds. Emrys Jones converted four of the tries and dropped a goal. G. Morgan scored an unconverted try for Aberavon.

NEATH'S CONVINCING SUCCESS.

Pontypool Beaten by 26 Points.

THE ALL BLACKS' CONSISTENCY.

(By " RECORDER.")

The All Blacks are worthy of the appelation, "Welsh Champions." They have vanquished all the leading clubs which have visited the Gnoll by, in the majority of instances, huge margins. They defeated Pontypool by almost a substantial a margin as they had previously beaten Llanelly and Aberavon, and their supremacy was not by any means exaggerated by the score. The Monmouthshire side were outclassed in every department with the exception of at full-back, where Neath lacked the services of Phil Lloyd, owing to illness. His deputy, M. Howells, played a plucky game, but frequently failed to find touch.

WELSH SELECTORS PRESENT.

The home three quarters were in their superb in the open and maintained their improvement in scrummaging. Tom Arthur and Hollingdale satisfied the selectors as to their fitness for inclusion against England; and now that Lemon most brilliant mood, which is sufficient comment, and it remains to be seen how they impressed Messrs. Gwyn Nicholls and Garrett, two of the "Big Five" who witnessed the match. They would certainly not fail to have been impressed by the brilliancy of Owen and Reynolds, who made their opposite numbers, Werrett and Gould, appear very third-rate. Werrett had a penchant for getting offside, which would prove very costly if he appeared in the national side. Reynolds gave an object lesson in pivotal play, varying his tactics, to the complete bewilderment of the opposition. His break through, particularly when he scored a try, electrified the crowd. As a club pair the Neath halves are easily the best in Wales, and it is only by their inclusion in a Trial that it can be shown how clever they are.

The Neath pack were, as usual, have seen Arthur Lemon play, they can have no justification for ignoring him any longer. His try on Saturday was unique in its conception and execution.

The scorers for Neath were Dan Jones, Daniels, Howie Jones, Tom Arthur, Reynolds and Lemon. Emrys Jones convert

91

Welsh international Tom Arthur led Neath in 1931/32. Again, they were very much in championship contention with a record of Played 45, Won 35, Drawn 3, Lost 7, Points For 559, Points Against 218. From left to right, back row: D.H. Davies, B. Gorman, W.H. Waring, J. Dummer. Fourth row: C. Heard, R. Gregory, Ald. J.B. Williams, W.J. Hoare ('Old Stager'), T. Williams, W. Cooper, T. Youatt. Third row: S. Evans (trainer), G. Bevan, D.H. Davies, G. Prosser, G. Hughes, G. Roberts, D.L. Thomas, A. Lemon, G. Hopkins, T. Hollingdale, T.H. Morgan, A.J. Mills. Second row: Supt. R.Davies, W.A. Griffiths (secretary), G. Daniels, D.Jones, P. Howells (chairman), T. Arthur (captain), G. Callard, A. Hickman, G. Moore, B.Sutcliffe (treasurer), T. Davies. Front row: P. Lloyd, C. Evans, W.J. Trew, G. Thomas.

Tom Arthur was in the Aberavon and Neath combined XV which lost 8-3 to South Africa on 28 November 1931. Policeman Arthur was probably Neath's finest inter-war forward as he earned 18 caps for Wales. From left to right, back row: Mr T.D. Griffiths, G. Prosser (N), A. Lemon (N), Supt Rhys Davies. Third row: Mr P. Howells, G. Hopkins (N), M. McGrath (A), T. Arthur (N), W. Vickery (A), E.M. Jenkins (A), Mr W.A. Griffiths. Second row: F. Nicholas (A), G. Moore (N), Cyril Griffiths (A – captain), P. Lloyd (N), G. Daniels (N), D. Jones (N). Front row: W. Selby (A), T. Harris (A).

Neath were among the first clubs to form a properly consti-
tuted Supporters' Club. With ex-international Glyn Stephens
as president, they ran trips to away games, organised raffles
and raised sufficient funds for the development of the new
Dressing Room Stand.

NEW CLUB-HOUSE OPENED
Neath Supporters' Successful Effort
By HOTSPUR.

Prominent sportsmen were present at
the Gnoll, Neath, last evening, when
Mr. D. M. Evans-Bevan, president of
the Neath R.F.C., in the absence of his
wife, opened the new grand stand clubhouse.

Alderman J. B. Williams presided,
and he was supported by members of
the Neath Committee and the Neath
Supporters' Club Committee.

Alderman Williams said that thanks
to the work of Mr. Glyn Stephens, the
originator of the pavilion scheme, they
saw that day the realisation of their
hopes and dreams.

Mr. D. M. Evans-Bevan started them
off with the sum of £100 and followed
that up with a further donation of £150.
(Applause.) He was a chip of the old
block and they in Neath were very
proud of him.

The Supporters' Club had worked very
hard to achieve their object, and he
could say, as president of the Supporters' Club, that they were very
grateful for every donation made, even
if it was only one shilling.

Mr. Glyn Stephens, in handing a copy
of the resolution of the Supporters'
Club, deciding to hand over the stand to
the Neath R.F.C., to Mr. Evans-Bevan,
said that without the financial assis-
tance given by Mr. Evans-Bevan, the
opening of that stand would not have
been possible.

Mr. D. M. Evans-Bevan said that he
hoped the new modern club house
would make better players, and that
they would play for Neath and for
Wales.

Seven Sisters policeman Gordon Hopkins took over as captain for 1932/33. Again, Neath
finished with an impressive record: Played 48, Won 32, Drawn 4, Lost 12, Points For 544,
Points Against 283. From left to right, back row: P. Howells, W.H. Davies, V. Friend, D.H.
Davies, D. Yapp, G. Hughes, G. Prosser, G. Lowry, J. Jenkins, D.R. Prosser, B. Gorman, W.
Cooper. Third row: B. Sutcliffe (treasurer), T.G. Jones, G. Thomas, R. Jones, F. Lewis, H.
Thomas, D.L. Thomas, T. Arthur, G. Watkins, T.H. Morgan, J. Dummer, A.J. Mills. Second
row: Supt R. Davies, T. Davies, D. Jones, P. Lloyd, W.A. Griffiths (secretary), G. Hopkins
(captain), G. Callard (chairman), G. Moore, C. Harris, W.H. Waring. Front row: S. Evans
(trainer), C. Evans, A. Hickman, G. Daniels, H. Thomas, C. Heard.

Rev. G.A.L. (Gareth) Evans was one of several clergymen to appear in Neath colours. He was a curate at St David's Church and the Rector of Neath, Gwilym Francis, who served on the Neath Committee, intoned from the pulpit one Sunday morning following a particularly 'warm' game against Aberavon, 'Now the day is over, Night is drawing nigh, Poor old Gareth Evans, Has a beefsteak on his eye.'

A.C. Walsh. Conor Walsh was a free-scoring wing. An Irishman from the Old Crescent club, he played two seasons for the Neath club and is probably the source of rumours which still circulate today that another Irish wing W.T. Joyce ('Lord Haw-Haw', the Nazi propagandist) played for Neath. Walsh's appearance at The Gnoll, together with that of Gloucester's A.T. Voyce, who played against Neath, helped make the 'link'!

Neath RFC Supporters Club Committee, 1930/31.

Among the many efforts attributable to the Supporters' Club was the introduction of the match programme. Weston-Super-Mare were popular visitors to The Gnoll as their ranks included many Welshmen who had crossed the Bristol Channel in search of work. This programme from 1931/32 indicates that Neath wore letters for identification although numbers came into use shortly afterwards.

D.M. Evans-Bevan was president of Neath RFC for over forty years. He had extensive mining interests in the locality and owned the Vale of Neath Brewery – Evans-Bevan ales were nearly as famous as the All Blacks!

Left: Dan Jones, Neath's flying winger, scored 59 tries for the club in 1928/29 and 73 in total (2 in Welsh trials, 6 for Glamorgan County and 6 in GWR internationals). He played for Wales against NSW Waratahs in 1927. *Right:* J.B. Williams served on the Neath Committee from the early 1900s and was chairman in 1913/14. He played cricket for Neath, served on the Supporters' Club Committee and became mayor in 1936.

Seven
Defying the Depression

During the deep inter-war depression, Neath like many Welsh clubs suffered from a veritable drain of players to the Rugby League and over fifty Neath players went north. Many, had they stayed, would surely have gone on to play for Wales. It is hardly surprising that the national XV did not enjoy a particularly productive time between the wars given the flood of internationals who switched codes. Neath's losses included internationals Ambrose Baker, Eddie Watkins, Eddie Williams, Dan Pascoe, Arthur Lemon, Gomer Hughes (via Penarth), Glyn Prosser, D.R. Prosser, Harold Thomas and Arthur Hickman. Hickman was arguably Neath's most talented all-round back of the inter-war period. A prolific try-scorer, he played wing, centre and outside half and was an excellent goal-kicker. The Blacks are often at their best when the chips are down and despite all their northern defections, the loss of players like Gwyn Thomas (who earned a Welsh trial from Leicester) who left to find employment in England and others who moved clubs (and jobs!) within South Wales, Neath followed their 1928/29 triumph by winning the Welsh championship in 1933/34 and again in 1934/35.

Twice-capped Arthur Hickman captained Neath to their second Welsh championship in 1933/34. Their record read: Played 50, Won 42, Drawn 1, Lost 7, Points For 653, Points Against 253. From left to right, back row: B. Sutcliffe (treasurer), S. Simmons, T.G. Jones, D. Yapp, B. Glover, J. John, P. Howells. Fourth row: A.R. Harris, J.S. George, D.H. Davies, F. Lewis, G. Hopkins, R. Jones, B. Morgan, G. Callard, Coun. J.T. Evans, Ald. J.B. Williams. Third row: S. Evans (trainer), A.J. Mills, G. Heavens, D.H. Davies, D.R. Prosser, D.L. Thomas, M. Rees, G. Prosser, H. Thomas, D. Jones, Coun. W.K. Owen, J. Dummer. Second row: D.M. Evans, G. Moore, G. Daniels, W.A. Griffiths (secretary), A. Hickman (captain), W.H. Waring (chairman), T.H. Morgan, G. Thomas, T. Davies. Front row: I. Davies, E. Youatt.

Welsh Schools cap Charlie Banfield played centre for Neath, but joined the rugby league drain where he won international honours.

Glyn Prosser (seated, third from left) was a-tough-as-teak forward from Glynneath. He and his brother D.R. became the first pair of Neath brothers to play for Wales. Here he is in the Wales XV which defeated New Zealand 13-12 in 1934/35.

Two leading Neath RFC committee men, Supt. Rhys Davies and Alderman W.K. Owen, as captured by a newspaper cartoonist.

NEATH RUGBY FOOTBALL CLUB

SEASON 1933/34   **CAPTAIN : ARTHUR HICKMAN**

Sept.	2	Skewen	W	27	0	H
	9	Resolven	W	16	8	H
	14	Pontypridd	W	9	0	H
	16	Aberavon	L	4	5	H
	23	Llanelly	L	8	12	A
	28	Morriston	W	14	0	A
	30	Maesteg	W	18	3	H
Oct.	2	W.J.Llewellyn's XV	W	24	6	H
	7	Aberavon	L	8	18	A
	9	Exeter	W	25	8	H
	14	Swansea	L	6	8	A
	19	Skewen	W	11	8	A
	21	Lydney	W	27	0	H
	28	Newport	W	14	9	A
Nov.	4	Cross Keys	W	15	0	A
	11	Glynneath	W	25	7	H
	18	Cardiff	L	3	6	A
	25	St. Mary's Hospital	W	9	6	H
Dec.	2	Resolven	W	14	0	A
	9	Swansea	P	P		H
	16	Llanelly	W	6	4	H
	23	Cardiff	W	18	8	H
	25	London Welsh	W	10	6	H
	26	Abertillery	W	17	3	H
	30	Pontypool	W	17	3	H
Jan.	6	Glynneath	W	4	0	A
	13	Devonport Services	W	11	6	A
	15	Newton Abbot	W	19	8	A
	16	Exeter	W	9	0	A
	20	*WALES nil ENGLAND 9 pts (at Cardiff)*				
	27	Aberavon	W	14	0	H
Feb.	3	*SCOTLAND 6 pts WALES 13 pts (at Murrayfield)*				
	3	Maesteg	W	22	7	A
	8	Swansea	W	8	6	A
	10	Penarth	W	20	6	H
	17	Llanelly	L	3	17	H
	24	Pontypool	L	3	8	A
Mar.	1	Swansea	W	12	6	H
	3	London Hospital	W	21	0	H
	8	Briton Ferry	W	13	11	H
	10	*WALES 13 pts IRELAND 11 pts (at Swansea)*				
	10	Lydney	W	14	3	A
	13	Penarth	W	10	0	A
	17	Bridgend	W	8	0	H
	22	Llanelly	W	9	6	H
	24	Aberavon	W	6	0	A
	29	Bath	W	20	3	H
	31	Cross Keys	W	21	5	H
Apr.	2	U.A.U.	W	26	8	H
	3	Bridgend	L	7	16	A
	5	Swansea	D	3	3	H
	7	Pontypridd	W	10	6	A
	14	Devonport Services	W	12	4	H
	21	Newport	W	3	0	H
	28	Abertillery	W	11	3	A
May	3	Pontardawe	W	19	4	H
				683	**264**	

Played	**52**
Won	**43**
Drawn	**1**
Lost	**8**

WELSH CHAMPIONS

Neath RFC, Welsh Champions, results 1933/34.

ABERTILLERY
EXTENDED
CHAMPIONS

But Neath Deserved to Win

	G.	T.	Pts.
Neath	1	2	11
Abertillery	0	1	3

Attendance, 1,500.

Exhilarating Rugby was seen at Abertillery on Saturday between Neath, the unofficial Welsh champions, and Abertillery.

The champions' victory was a tardy one, their 11 points being registered towards the end of the game, though, be it said, in less than that number of minutes.

A rally which resulted in a deserved try was the only reply that Abertillery were able to make.

Up to the time Neath scored their first try, and in the first half particularly, Abertillery shared the spoils in attack and defence. Abertillery's line had its escapes, but so did Neath's.

After the interval the All Blacks, through the superiority their forwards established in the scrums and the speed of their backs, repeatedly launched attacks on the Abertillery line. Once it had been crossed the defence crumbled, and Neath reaped the reward which, it must be conceded, was deservedly theirs.

PLUCKY RESISTANCE

Abertillery put up a great resistance and played more convincing football than they have for a considerable period. The outstanding man was G. Moore, the Neath centre. A great attacking back, he scored two tries.

Powell served Abertillery well, especially in the first half, but he took less watching than the elusive Youatt for Neath.

Despite his youth, Ken Green, the secondary school boy international, at full-back for Abertillery, stood up magnificently to the Neath attacks, and acquitted himself in a manner that would have been creditable to a more experienced player.

Following Moore's two tries R. Jones was sent over by Youatt for a try which Hickman converted. Subsequently Pugh scored for Abertillery. Teams:—

Abertillery: K. Green; G. Woodhouse, H. Richardson, L. Murray, A. E. Williams; C. Powell, G. Gimblett; M. Meek, G. Morgan, T. Pugh, T. Richards, T. Sayers, E. Lloyd, R. Fildes, W. Watkins.

Neath: G. Thomas; D. H. Davies, G. Daniels, G. Moore, I. Davies; E. Youatt, A. Hickman; T. Arthur, D. R. Prosser, D. L. Thomas, M. Rees, D. M. Evans, G. Hopkins, H. Thomas, R. Jones.

Neath are the Champions

BY "OLD STAGER"

Only one change occurs in the unofficial Welsh Rugby championship table as a consequence of the games of the last week, Aberavon climbing to the eighth place at the expense of Swansea.

The season is now too far advanced for there to be any material changes in the placings, and the championship must be secured by Neath, with Llanelly as runners-up.

The present placings are:—

	P.	W.	D.	L.	Points F.	A.	Per-cent'ge
Neath	49	40	1	8	629	257	82.65
Llanelly	44	34	3	7	572	195	80.68
Bridgend	43	31	3	9	538	201	75.58
Pontypool	46	28	7	11	411	212	68.47
Cross Keys	41	23	7	11	405	225	64.63
Cardiff	41	23	2	16	358	267	58.53
Newport	41	22	3	16	262	240	57.31
Aberavon	41	22	2	17	383	232	56.09
Swansea	39	20	3	16	366	214	55.12
Penarth	38	20	1	17	304	255	53.94
Abertillery	30	17	2	16	274	229	51.22

Above: Final championship table, 1933/34. *Left:* The 1933/34 championship was clinched at Abertillery Park.

RUGBY FOOTBALL

CHAMPIONSHIP TABLE

Aberavon Runners Up to Neath

By "OLD STAGER"

Nothing that can happen between now and the end of the extended season can affect the final placings on the unofficial Welsh Rugby championship table or the all-Welsh table.

Neath, for the second year in succession, are the unofficial Welsh champions, with Aberavon as runners-up and Swansea and Cardiff in the third and fourth positions respectively.

The order of those placings is slightly varied on the all-Welsh table, Aberavon occupying the leading position, with Neath as runners-up. Aberavon take the lead solely as a result of their victory over the All Blacks on Monday.

The final placings on the unofficial championship table are:—

	P.	W.	D.	L.	Points F.	A.	Per-cent'ge
Neath	44	32	1	11	409	203	73.86
Aberavon	48	33	3	12	507	217	71.87
Swansea	42	26	5	11	433	231	67.85
Cardiff	44	25	5	14	389	244	62.50
Abertillery	45	26	4	15	355	216	62.22
Llanelly	46	27	3	16	444	310	61.95
Bridgend	47	26	5	16	418	292	60.63
Pontypool	42	21	2	16	505	240	59.52
Newport	45	20	7	18	337	277	54.65
Cross Keys	38	15	5	18	285	256	46.05
Penarth	39	12	5	22	258	332	37.17

Right: Final championship table, 1934/35 – Neath were back-to-back champions.

NEATH RUGBY FOOTBALL CLUB

SEASON 1934/35   **CAPTAIN : GLYN DANIELS**

Sept.	1	Glynneath	W	15	0	H
	8	Skewen	W	25	0	H
	15	Cardiff	L	3	6	A
	22	Cross Keys	W	13	0	H
	29	Aberavon	W	26	11	H
Oct.	1	Pontypool	L	3	6	A
	6	Bridgend	W	3	0	A
	13	Pontypool	W	14	3	H
	18	Swansea	W	8	3	A
	20	Cross Keys	W	11	9	H
	27	Maesteg	W	9	0	H
Nov.	3	Newport	L	3	8	A
	10	Llanelly	W	11	3	H
	17	Cardiff	L	3	5	H
	24	Bridgend	L	3	11	H
Dec.	1	Penarth	L	0	3	A
	8	Aberavon	L	3	6	A
	15	Pontypridd	W	22	0	H
	22	Swansea	D	0	0	H
	25	London Welsh	W	14	5	H
	26	Abertillery	W	6	3	H
	27	Bath	W	13	3	A
	29	Llanelly	L	9	14	A
Jan.	5	Maesteg	W	9	6	A
	12	Penarth	W	5	0	H
	19	*ENGLAND 3 pts WALES 3 pts (at Twickenham)*		9		
	26	Aberavon	W	6	5	H
Feb.	2	*WALES 10 pts SCOTLAND 6 pts (at Cardiff)*				
	9	Bridgend	W	16 0	0	H
	16	Aberavon	C	-	-	A
	23	Devonport Services	W	12	6	A
	25	Redruth	L	0	14	A
Mar.	2	Llanelly	W	5	3	H
	7	Briton Ferry	W	20	3	H
	9	*IRELAND 9 pts WALES 3 pts (at Belfast)*				
	9	Bath	C	-	-	H
	14	Pontypridd	W	8	5	A
	16	London Hospital	W	29	5	H
	21	Bath	W	11	5	H
	23	Llanelly	W	3	0	A
	30	Swansea	L	3	11	A
Apr.	4	Skewen	W	20	3	A
	6	Old Paulines	W	23	3	H
	11	Swansea	W	5	3	H
	13	Newport	W	9	8	H
	20	Devonport Services	W	11	5	H
	22	Middlesex Hospital	W	16	10	H
	23	Abertillery	W	3	0	A
	27	Bridgend	W	9	8	A
	29	Aberavon	L	3	8	A
May	4	Glynneath	W	3	0	H

	446	**210**

Played	46
Won	34
Drawn	1
Lost	11

WELSH CHAMPIONS

Neath RFC, Welsh Champions, results 1934/35

Neath the Welsh Champions Again

Vital Points in Final Minutes

Two Men Sent off in Aberavon Duel

GWYN MOORE'S TRIUMPH

TRY SAVES THE SITUATION

(By " Alert ")

NEATH have closed a season full of ups and downs, and finished on a top note by becoming the unofficial Welsh champions for the second season in succession. This achievement was brought about as a result of their thrilling victory over Bridgend last Saturday by nine points to eight points.

It was a great game of Rugby, played in a sporting spirit, despite the issues involved, and attracted one of the largest crowds of the season. Neath's capabilities as a team were proved beyond a shadow of doubt by the fact that they won after being eight points in arrears. Few teams could bring off such a spectacular victory against a team like Bridgend on their own ground, and all credit must go to the All Blacks for their triumph, which was achieved through clean and open football. In particular, praise must be accorded to Gwyn Moore, the Neath captain, who burst through for the winning try a few minutes from time. He beat four men to crown a magnificent effort, and was given a reception almost unparalleled in the history of Welsh Rugby. Although the game was unfinished spectators rushed on the field to shake him by the hand.

WORTHY WINNERS

Neath were fully worthy of the honours and had the territorial advantage nearly all the way. Their strength at forward was the main reason for this, coupled with the powerful work of Gwyn Moore and Gwyn Thomas at centre.

The first Bridgend score caused some comment, as Parfitt was considered to be offside when he took a pass intended for a Neath man and sent C. V. Jeffreys over for W. J. Chilcott to convert.

This was a set-back for Neath, but their position was worsened when Chris Matthews crossed with an unconverted try after one of his typical speedy runs.

DETERMINATION AND TEAMWORK

It was then that Neath showed what they were made of. They played with fine determination and teamwork, and after the Bridgend side revealed themselves a beaten team, D. H. Davies and Harold Thomas scored tries.

It was hard going afterwards, but Gwyn Moore gave Neath the lead and the championship.

The Neath forwards worked particularly hard, and D. L. Thomas, Harold Thomas, Emrys Hill and D. M. Evans were good leaders, whilst all played their part well.

D. H. Davies was the cleverer of the two wings, and Randell Parker

Neath won at Bridgend to clinch the 1934/35 championship title.

Bert Sutcliffe, treasurer of Neath RFC.

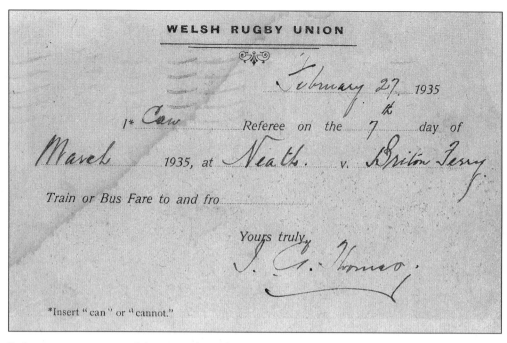

WELSH RUGBY UNION

February 27, 1935

I* *can* Referee on the 7th day of *March* 1935, at *Neath* v. *Briton Ferry*

Train or Bus Fare to and fro

Yours truly,
J. G. Thomas.

*Insert " can " or " cannot."

Referee appointment card from 1934/35. The reverse reads simply 'Walter E. Rees, Neath' – post thus addressed was able to find its way to the WFU secretary from all over the rugby world.

Bert Gorman, secretary of Neath Rugby Supporters' Club.

Neath RFC, 1935/36. Final record: Played 48, Won 30, Drawn 3, Lost 15, Points For 455, Points Against 252. From left to right, back row: W.H.Davies, A.E. Freethy, C. Challinor, A. McCarley, T.H. Morgan, C. Roberts, C. Lewis, W. Davies, B. Gorman, P. Howells. Third row: S. Evans (trainer), Coun. J.S. George, D.H. Davies, R. Jones, H. Thomas, V. Phillips, L. James, E. Morgan, W.H. Waring. Second row: Ald. J.B. Williams, G. Callard, J. Sargeant, W.A. Griffiths (secretary), G. Moore (captain), T. Davies (chairman), D.L. Thomas, Ald. W.K. Owen, H.M. Powell, B. Sutcliffe (treasurer). Front row: E. Walters, J.S. Gratton, S. Harris, D. Parker, W. Lewis, I. Owen.

That most dashing of centres Gwyn Moore was a mainstay of the Neath team almost throughout the 1930s until injury curtailed his career. His quality is best illustrated by the many tries he unselfishly created for his wing three-quarters. He captained Neath in 1935/36, was travelling reserve for Wales on several occasions and represented a Wales XV v. The Rest. However, that elusive cap was never his probably because the selectors found it difficult to comprehend that Neath had backs as well as forwards.

THRILLS IN BIG GAME AT ABERAVON

NEW ZEALAND WIN THE MATCH BY OPPORTUNISM

GALLANT FORWARDS

By PENDRAGON.

Neath and Aberavon ... 3pts.
New Zealand ... 13pts.

IT is not at all difficult to supply a reason for the failure of the combined Neath and Aberavon side to beat New Zealand, even though they secured the upper hand in scrummaging.

Stumbling blocks to success were the indecision which was shown at three-quarter, the tendency to "bunch," and the weakness which was displayed by centres who persisted in running towards the touchlines instead of seeking to break through.

There was also the aspect that Gwyn Thomas did not appear to be at all happy at outside half, for while he did some valuable kicking he was not a successful weaver of openings.

Undoubtedly the combined side gave the All Blacks one of the hardest matches of the tour. They rattled them forward, and they were more effective than them at inside half, where M Baker played a surprisingly good game; whereas Sadler, usually one of the liveliest of the New Zealanders, was less effective than he had been on any other Welsh ground.

The combined side had some unfortunate moments of indecision. I suppose that Powell was as fast as any of his opponents, but he did not use his speed as well as he could have done, and there was one occasion early in the game when he hesitated with the line almost open to him.

Still Powell made a better wing than J Bevan, one of his strongest points being his close marking of Ball. That player broke away cleverly to pave the way for Griffiths's try, but I fancy that this movement should have been pulled up for a knock-on.

A REMARKABLE TRY.

I have often remarked upon the capacity which these tourists have shown for suddenly turning defence into attack. Frequently they have scored tries from positions of danger to themselves, and when Ball made the running for that second try it was the combined side, not the New Zealanders, who looked like getting over. Intelligent backing up, sureness of handling, and cleverness in picking up a rolling ball when on the run, were things which helped the New Zealand backs to win a match in which they suffered some uncomfortable periods.

Their speed and their wonderful quickness off the mark were other attributes which made for success; yet their forward play was quite ordinary. Here, at all events, they met their match. In the circumstances it may be counted surprising that only one of that valiant pack, Glyn Prosser, has found his way into the Welsh side to oppose New Zealand at Cardiff.

The success gained by Neath and Aberavon in heeling was a distinct tribute to the virtues of the "hooking" of Tonna Morgan, while the enthusiasm which was shown in the rushes and the loose melees testified to the value of Glyn Prosser's leadership.

Altogether it was a splendidly knitted pack, worthy of better support than it received. Walter Vickery and H. Matthews did prodigies of good work in the line-out, while the stockily built Neath forward, D. M. Evans, was a glutton in the loose.

HONOURS SHARED.

Sharing the honours with Baker, so far as the "combined" backs were concerned, was T. O. James, who made but one mistake throughout the afternoon, that consisting of failure to catch the ball on the edge of his own line. Speaking generally, James was better than Gilbert.

Jack Thomas was the best of the Neath-Aberavon threequarters, but, as I have shown, it was a line which was generally lacking in constructive ideas.

In the territorial sense, Neath and Aberavon had more of the game, and having regard to the high quality of the opposition, they can be congratulated.

Neath & Aberavon played New Zealand in December 1935. The Combined XV's forwards matched the All Blacks but the backs, handicapped by the late withdrawal of the injured Gwyn Moore, were not up to the mark. The match was refereed by former Neath captain Dai Hiddlestone. At half time, a young supporter ventured onto the field and presented him with a bunch of flowers which he rather ungraciously threw on the ground!

Emlyn Walters was a free-scoring centre for Neath. He also flirted with Pontypridd and later earned international honours at rugby league.

Eight
Jubilee celebrations and the gathering storm

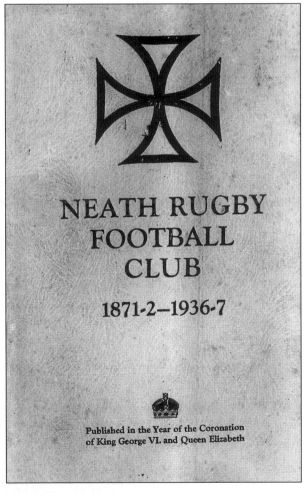

Sixty-five years on from their birth, Neath RFC celebrated their jubilee in 1936/37. To mark the occasion, the Supporters' Club produced a special jubilee brochure which included *inter alia* an article by Sam Clarke and a brief outline of the club's development by a local antiquarian Donald H. Jones who had unearthed the original reference to Neath's game at Swansea in 1872.

Neath RFC, *c.* 1936.

Neath's jubilee captain was second row Harold Thomas. The following season, he too joined the R.L. exodus and won international honours in both codes.

In 1936/37, the Blacks finished with 20 wins, 7 draws and 12 defeats from 39 games. From left to right, back row: W. Davies, D.L. Daniel, D.L. Thomas, W.J. Jones, Ted Ward. Middle row: S. Evans (trainer), G. Moore, E. Morgan, D. Evans, H. Thomas (captain), H.M. Powell, C. Challinor, I. Owen. Front row: E. Walters, D. Parker, P. Thomas.

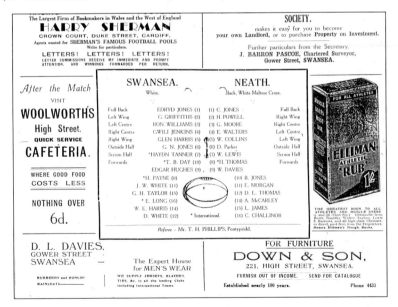

Other clubs followed Neath's example in setting up supporters' organisations. When Neath visited St Helen's, Swansea, in September 1936, where they won 3-0, the programme indicated that there were five internationals in the Neath pack that day – skipper Harold Thomas, Eddie Morgan (later to become a Lion from Swansea), D.L. Thomas, Allen McCarley and Cyril Challinor. The referee T. Harold Phillips settled in Neath and served on the Glamorgan County Committee.

Team group, 1937/38 – captain D.L. Thomas. David Leyshon Thomas, like his brother Harold, was capped by Wales. First the Prossers, then the Thomases, later the Llewellyns: brothers and forwards all.

Harold Powell was a try-scoring wing. He joined Neath from the 'Shoppoes' and then played for Swansea before returning to The Gnoll after the war, where he enjoyed several stints as chairman.

Programme from the Neath-Swansea return fixture at The Gnoll in March 1937. Note the 5.00pm kick-off and the programme number 8,991, which suggests that a large attendance was expected! Was the weather fine or were supporters warmly clad in the 2 guinea overcoat available from Zeiler's?

Cheaper raincoats were on offer at Phillips Brothers on The Square. Among the advertisers were the President's Vale of Neath Brewery and The Cambrian Hotel, which doubled as the headquarters of the Glamorgan County RFC.

Thanks largely to the dedication of masters such as Les Smith, Neath Schoolboys enjoyed a high profile as this advertisement suggests.

Neath's sixty-fifth anniversary was marked by a game against Oxford University. Included in the Neath team was Ted Ward of Ammanford who joined Wigan R.L. and enjoyed a brilliant career in which he represented the Great Britain R.L. team.

TEAMS FOR THE JUBILEE MATCH

OXFORD UNIVERSITY XV.		NEATH	
(1) H. D. Freakes	Full Back	(1) Cliff Jones	Full Back
Threequarters :		**Threequarters :**	
(2) C. P. Mayhew	Right Wing	(2) H. Powell	Right Wing
(22) L. C. Carrel	Right Centre	(3) E. Walters	Right Centre
(4) J. C. Stevens	Left Centre	(4) Gwyn Moore	Left Centre
(5) W. N. Renwick	Left Wing	(5) E. Ward	Left Wing
Half-Backs :		**Half-Backs :**	
(6) A. L. Dawkins	Outside	(6) W. Idwal Davies	Outside
(23) R. T. Campbell	Scrum	(7) Dai Parker	Scrum
Forwards :		**Forwards :**	
(9) J. A. Brett (capt.)		(8) Harold Thomas (capt.)	
(16) R. J. Pollok-Morris		(9) E. Morgan	
(17) R. G. P. Almond		(10) Denver Evans	
(12) C. J. Laubscher		(11) W. Davies	
(13) B. J. Stubbings		(12) Les. James	
(7) H. M. Hughes		(14) D. L. Thomas	
(14) B. T. Bloxham		(15) W. J. Jones	
(21) T. Carrel		(16) C. Challinor	
Referee : Mr. A. E. Freethy		Kick-off 5.15 p.m.	

Neath RFC, 1937/38. From left to right, back row: W.D. Davies, L. James, Ted Cook, W.G. Bevan, W.J. Jones, C. Challinor, A. McCarley. Middle row: E. Walters, J. Sargeant, D.L. Thomas (captain), W.T. Davies, I. Owen, S. Evans (trainer). Front row: W.L. Thomas, W.E. Jones, M. Clement.

Allen McCarley in action at the back of the line-out for Wales at Murrayfield in 1938, when he scored two tries. McCarley was elected captain for 1939/40, but a leg injury sustained the previous season prevented him from playing and Neath were consequently skippered by prop Bill Davies in their 'wartime season'.

NEWPORT			NEATH
Full Back	W. G. Legge—1	1—I. Owen	Full Back
Right Wing	K. James—2	2—J. Sargeant	Right Wing
Right Centre	J. H. Dunn—3	3—S. Harris	Right Centre
Left Centre	R. Allin—4	4—T. Ward	Left Centre
Left Wing	J. C. Adams—5	5—E. Walters	Left Wing
Inside Half	A. R. Tovey—7	6—D. Parker	Inside Half
Outside Half	R. Wade—6	7—W. E. Jones	Outside Half

Referee :

Mr. W. J. Davies, Llanelly

Kick-off 3.30 p.m.

Forwards (from)	J. R. Evans—10	8—D. Evans	Forwards (from)
	T. J. Rees—11	9—E. Morgan	
	W. Travers—12	10—W. Davies	
	J. C. Jerman—14	11—Harold Thomas (Capt)	
	A. J. Bale—15	12—J. Cole	
	V. J. Law—16	14—L. James	
	A. Rowe—17	15—B. Jones	
	M. Chatwin—18	16—A. McCarley	
	R. Phillips	D. L. Thomas	

Neath lined up against Newport in 1937 and this programme extract indicates the strength of the teams on show.

W.T. (Wil Twm) Davies was a bustling, goal-kicking centre from Abercrave who made his mark in 1937/38.

W.L. (Wil Dic) Thomas was a scrum-half from Ystradgynlais who was an effective foil for Willie Jones.

Prop forward Eddie Morgan joined Neath from Abercrave and he played two seasons at The Gnoll before joining the old Swansea Borough Police force. At the same time he exchanged the black of Neath for the white of Swansea and, having earned his Welsh cap, went on the British Lions tour to South Africa in 1938.

SEASON 1938/39			CAPTAIN : W.E.JONES			
Sept.	3	Resolven	W	36	0	H
	10	Weston-Super-Mare	W	16	3	H
	17	Guy's Hospital	W	15	8	H
	24	Cardiff	L	6	11	A
Oct.	1	Swansea	L	3	6	A
	8	Pontypool	W	20	8	H
	15	Aberavon	W	12	6	H
	22	Leicester	L	13	20	A
	29	Bridgend	W	20	5	H
Nov.	5	Cross Keys	L	9	13	A
	12	Bridgend	W	13	3	A
	19	Llanelly	W	9	3	H
	26	Swansea	L	6	9	A
Dec.	3	Maesteg	D	4	4	A
	10	Llanelly	L	5	14	A
	17	Bristol	W	19	6	H
	24	London Welsh	C			H
	26	Abertillery	W	21	6	H
	31	Penarth	W	8	3	A
Jan.	7	Weston-Super-Mare	L	7	8	A
	14	Maesteg	W	5	0	H
	21	*ENGLAND 3 pts WALES nil (at Twickenham)*				
	21	Abertillery	C			A
	28	Bridgend	L	3	5	A
Feb.	4	*WALES 11 pts SCOTLAND 3 pts (at Cardiff)*				
	4	Bath	D	9	9	A
	11	Swansea	L	4	5	A
	18	Penarth	W	32	3	H
	25	Aberavon	W	5	3	A
Mar.	4	Swansea	W	9	5	H
	11	*Ireland nil WALES 7 pts (at Belfast)*				
	11	Resolven	W	14	0	A
	13	Llanelly	L	6	13	A
	18	Cross Keys	W	16	7	H
	20	Oxford University	L	6	10	H
	25	Newport	L	5	19	A
Apr.	1	Llanelly	L	0	8	H
	3	Pontypool	L	3	6	A
	8	Ebbw Vale	W	18	9	H
	10	Nuneaton	W	25	11	H
	11	Bridgend	W	26	16	A
	15	Bath	W	20	3	H
	19	Ebbw Vale	L	9	18	A
	22	Briton Ferry	W	9	8	H
	24	Cardiff	D	0	0	H
	29	Newport	W	8	3	H
May	6	Abertillery	W	7	3	A
				481	**300**	
		Played	**42**			
		Won	**24**			
		Drawn	**3**			
		Lost	**15**			

Neath's 1938/39 season shows that the fixture list had developed into something akin to post-war times – a list which served them well until the introduction of leagues.

Left: Cyril Challinor was a tough back-row forward who joined Neath from Crynant. He won his only Welsh cap at Twickenham in 1938. His best years were probably lost to the war, but he resumed play in 1945 and later served on the Neath committee. *Right:* Hooker Denver Evans was a regular member of the Neath pack in the late 1930s. The Brynamman product enjoyed the dubious distinction of being sent off in successive games in 1939/40, escaping suspension due to the 'unofficial' nature of the games against Cardiff and Swansea.

Neath Schools won the Dewar Shield in 1938/39 under the captaincy of Morlais Thomas, who established himself at senior level and captained Neath in 1948/49. Back rower Thomas represented Wales against the New Zealand Kiwis in the Victory International in 1945/46.

W.E. Jones
Captain of Neath R.F.C.
1938 - 39

Carmarthen product W.E. Jones (above and opposite top) played a few games for Llanelli but in 1936/37 he joined Neath as a left-footed outside half with a penchant for dropping goals. He made a single post-war appearance for Neath and nearly won the game for them against the New Zealand Kiwis in 1945, marginally failing with two drop-goal attempts which would have given Neath victory.

W.E. Jones played for Wales in a wartime 'Red Cross' international against England. He never won a full cap and is better known for his cricketing exploits as part of the Glamorgan team which first won the County Championship in 1948.

Neath forwards on the rampage at Swansea, October 1938.

NEATH'S FINE TEAM-WORK AGAINST CARDIFF

By WATCHMAN

BRINGING with them to the Gnoll last evening the reputation of having placed themselves secure as champions of Wales, together with the seven players who won the Middlesex seven-a-side tournament at Twickenham last Saturday, Cardiff were lucky to depart without being defeated by the All Blacks.

As the result of the poor showing of Neath in recent games owing to depleted sides caused by injuries to a batch of players, Cardiff were being strongly tipped to swamp Neath. The position was altered completely by the brilliant team-work shown by the All Blacks, who were far more worthy of carrying away the honours than the champions.

Old-time rugby seemed to have returned to the Gnoll, where 5,000 rugby followers were treated to one of the best games ever seen between the clubs and certainly the outstanding match seen at Neath for quite a long time. Despite the fact that no score was registered there was one thrilling movement after another, and the All Blacks surprised even their own supporters by a performance which will be talked about for seasons to come.

SCHOOLBOY'S TRIUMPH.

Most memorable feature will be the personal triumph of J. Matthews, the Bridgend Secondary schoolboy centre, over Wilfred Wooller. Time and again the schoolboy tackled Wooller in deadly fashion and swerved past him with comparative ease.

Matthews shows every promise of being the natural successor to Wooller in the Welsh side on his performance last evening.

Cardiff missed a batch of opportunities to score and Wooller failed a few times to kick penalties and drop goals, but his kicking generally was eclipsed by the way W. E Jones played. The best attempt to land a penalty came from Jones, whose kick from the half-way line just fell short of the cross-bar. The kicking of Wooller and Jones when defending their respective lines probably prevented many tries being scored.

W. T. Jones and Glyn Jones, the wings, crossed the line more than once but were recalled.

At the base of the scrum, W. L. Thomas had the better of W. G. Morgan; while at full-back D. G. Davies proved to be a greater unit than D. Brown. Davies played a game which ranks him as one of the best full-backs in the country to-day.

Surprise of the Neath pack was Brian Jones, Briton Ferry, as winging forward.

Neath's last official 'big game' of 1938/39 was a 0-0 draw at home to Cardiff. A young Bridgend County School centre by the name of Jack Matthews bottled up the considerable threat of Cardiff's Wilf Wooller and was destined for a bright career.

120

A worthy successor to the refereeing mantle of Albert Freethy was Ivor David, who controlled the Calcutta Cup matches of 1938 and 1939. He later refereed a further 12 internationals after the war and was much in demand for Varsity matches, touring games and trials. Ivor David played full back for Cimla RFC and cricket for several local teams including Cimla CC.

W. Arthur Griffiths served as honorary secretary from 1930 until 1946 and again from 1949 to 1971.

NEATH RUGBY WIN.

Neath scored a convincing win over an R.A.F. team in a Boxing Day match at the Gnoll ground, Neath, by two converted goals, six tries, 28 pts, to one converted goal, one try, 8 pts.

Neath's tries were scored by Bleddyn Williams (2), W. Jones (2), W. Thomas and G. Harry. Granville Jones converted two. Cunliffe and Plumpton scored tries for the R.A.F., Treharne converting one.

Ted Ward at centre and Bleddyn Williams and W. Thomas, the halves, were outstanding for Neath, whose threequarter play reached a good standard. The R.A.F. were strong in the loose forward rushes but lacked support behind.

On 3 September 1939, the WFU ordered its clubs to cease fixtures owing to the outbreak of war but four weeks later they relented and accepted that localised fixtures might resume on an unofficial basis. During the 'Phoney War', Neath played almost a full fixture list which included an unprecedented 6 wins over Swansea. Only 5 games were played in 1940/41 and 3 in 1941/42. All were won, including this match against the RAF. Neath's outside-half that day was Bleddyn Williams, while Ted Ward turned out at centre courtesy of the wartime rugby league amnesty.

Jack Matthews and Bleddyn Williams, Cardiff, Wales and British Lions centres par excellence, both also played for Neath.

Ossie Jones of Resolven played for Neath, St Helens RLFC and for the Welsh Guards.

The great Welsh full-back Vivian Jenkins played for Neath while on vacation in December 1939. 'Guest' players were sometimes introduced for wartime games when permit restrictions did not apply.

A UNIVERSITY XV. v. WELSH GUARDS (T.B.). Wednesday Nov. 5, 1941.

UNIVERSITY XV.	RUGBY	Welsh Guards (Training Batt.
1 J. R. BRIDGER (Rugby & Clare)	Full Back	1 O. JONES (Neath and Wigan
2 H. E. WATTS (Downside and Peterhouse)	Left Wing	2 VAUGHAN
3 B. G. CANGLEY (Felsted and Trinity Hall)	Left Centre	3 L./Cpl. PIMBLETT (St. Helens
4 A. D. THOMSON (Stowe & Caius)	Right Centre	4 2nd/Lt. P. R. H. HASTIN (Capt.
5 R. H. WHITWORTH (Cheadle & King's)	Right Wing	5 L./Cpl. ROWLANDS (Mountain Ash
6 G. T. WRIGHT (Kingswood & Queens')	Stand-off	6 L./Cpl. BANFIELD (Neath and Wigan
7 J. K. HARDY (Loretto & Pembroke)	Scrum	7 †Sgt. H. TANNER (Wales
8 J. A. DEW (Tonbridge & St. Catharine's)		8 2nd/Lt. F. BOLTON (Richmond
9 P. MALINS (Coventry and Downing)		9 JEFFERIES (Llanelly
10 A. M. WHITTINGTON (St. Paul's and St. John's)		10 Sgt. WILLIAMS (Neath
11 R. P. LISTER (Marlborough & Trinity)	Forwards	11 Sgt. BROWN (Glamorgan Police
12 P. K. LEDGER (Sherborne & St. Catharine's)		12 Sgt. DAVIS (Glamorgan Police
13 M. SHIRLEY (Cheadle and Queens')		13 †L./Cpl. WILLIAMS (Cardiff and Wigan
14 F. G. J. HAYHOE (Selhurst G.S. & Trinity Hall)		14 C.S.M. FISHER (Wasp
15 R. P. SINCLAIR (Bedford & Trinity Hall)	Referee	15 A. N. OTHER
	L. H. ELLIOTT.	† Signifies International.

Printed and Published by Metcalfe & Co., Ltd., for the C.U.R.U.F.C.

The restricted wartime rugby programme saw many ad-hoc matches. When Cambridge University played the Welsh Guards on 5 November 1942 the Guards fielded three Neath men in Charlie Banfield, Sgt Williams and Ossie Jones alongside the great Hadyn Tanner and back rower Gwyn Williams, the eldest of the Taffs Well brothers.

Records of Captains of the 1st. XV.

1871 -2	Dr. T. P. Whittington	1913-14	T. C. Lloyd.
1872-84	No record	1914-15	J. Pullman *elected.*
1884-85	A. T. Williams	15-19	W A R .
85-86	S. S. Clarke.	19-20	W. Hopkins.
6- 7	do.	20-21	L. Gwyn Thomas.
7- 8	do.	21-22	R. V. Hill.
8- 9	H. A. Bowen	22-23	J. Jones.
89-90	Dr. E. V. Pegge.	23-24	Ivor Jones
90-91	do.	24-25	D. Hiddlestone.
1- 2	do.	25-26	Jim John.
2- 3	G. D. Trick	26-27	D. Pascoe & D. Jones
3- 4	do.	27-28	G. Edwards
4- 5	C. Steer.	28-29	T. Evans.
5- 6	do.	29-30	do.
6- 7	W. Jones.	30-31	T. Hollingdale.
7- 8	do.	31-32	T. Arthur
8- 9	do.	32-33	G. Hopkins.
1899-1900	Joe Davies	33-34	A. Hickman.
1900- 1	W. Jones.	34-35	Glyn Daniels.
1- 2	do.	35-36	Gwyn Moore.
2- 3	D. H. Davies	36-37	H. Thomas.
3- 4	Howell Jones	37-38	D. L. Thomas.
4- 5	do.	38-39	W. E. Jones.
5- 6	W. Jones.	39-40	A. McCarley *elected.*
6- 7	do.		
7- 8	do.		
8- 9	do.		
9-10	Frank Rees.		
10-11	do.		
11-12	W. J. Perry		
12-13	F. David		

Neath RFC, Captains' Board from 1871 to 1940.

Neath & District Players who have gained Senior International Caps

Name.	Period.	No. of Caps.
T. Arthur	1927—1933	18
A. Baker	1921-22	5
J. Birch (x)	1911	2
C. Challinor	1939	1
S. S. Clarke	1882—1887	2
D. H. Davies	1904	1
Howell Davies	1912	2
D. Edwards (*Glynneath*)	1921	1
G. Gethin	1913	1
A. Hickman	1930—1933	2
D. Hiddlestone	1922—1924	5
T. Hollingdale	1927—1930	6
F. Hutchinson	1894—1896	3
Dan Jones	1927	1
Harold Jones	1929	2
Howell Jones	1904	1
Arthur Lemon	1929—1933	13
T. C. Lloyd	1909—1914	7
A. McCarley	1938	3
E. V. Pegge	1891	1
F. Perrett	1912—1913	5
W. Perry (x)	1911	1
D. R. Prosser	1934	2
Glyn Prosser	1934—1935	4
J. Pullman	1910	1
G. Stephens (*)	1912—1919	10
D. L. Thomas	1937	1
Harold Thomas	1936—1937	6
E. Watkins	1924	4
Eddie Williams	1921—1925	2

(x)   denotes when Wales won the "triple crown".

* Captained Wales 1919

Neath RFC Internationals, 1871-1945.

NEATH'S LIVELY FORM

CARDIFF BEATEN ON THE GNOLL

Neath and Cardiff met on the Gnoll on Saturday afternoon, in the game which was postponed during Warship Week, and after a sparkling encounter, Neath won by one converted goal, one dropped goal, two penalty goals, 15 pts., to two converted goals, 10pts.

Considering the difficulties in fielding a full side during wartime the match reached a remarkably high standard, and both sides made every effort to throw the ball about. The run of the play was fairly even throughout, and Cardiff possessing a more thrustful three-quarter line, were dangerous until the final whistle. Rosser and Cleaver, their halves, co-operated very successfully, and if the forwards had been able to get the ball back more frequently, it is doubtful whether the All Blacks would have won. They actually owed their victory to the consistent kicking of W. E. Jones, who altogether was responsible for twelve of their fifteen points.

There were some familiar faces in the Neath rear and forward divisions, notably W. T. Jones and M. Clement on the wings, and W. Davies, D. Lewis and C. Challinor among the forwards. W. L. Thomas played his usual steady game at inside-half.

Neath went ahead soon after the start, when W. E. Jones, making use of a good opportunity, dropped a neat goal. Cardiff fought back strongly, and following splendid work by the backs and a smart interception, Jack Matthews touched down under the posts for W. E. Tamplin to convert. Cardiff were clearly superior in the ensuing exchanges and improved their position when Bleddyn Williams raced over after some smart inter-passing. W. E. Tamplin converted again, and this closed the scoring in the first half. On the resumption W. E. Jones kicked two penalty goals to equalise the scores, and added the extra points to a try scored by D. P. Jones from a scrum right on the Cardiff line in the closing

NEATH'S HOLIDAY RUGBY

LIVELY GAME WITH R.A.F.

There was a lively exhibition of rugby on the Gnoll Ground on Easter Monday afternoon between a Neath XV. and an R.A.F. XV. which the former won in comfortable style by 16 points to nil. The proceeds were in aid of the War Comforts Fund of the Mayor of Neath.

While there was a war-time atmosphere about the game, at times flashes of old-time brilliance were displayed, and the large crowd had sufficient compensation in seeing a game after such a long period of enforced activity to be too critical.

Neath were clearly the better balanced side, and after setting up a good first half supremacy, forced home their advantage in the later period to good purpose. There were many familiar faces in the Neath team which called back reminiscences of better days, and to see W. E. Jones and W. L. Thomas together at the base of the scrum was entirely refreshing.

The R.A.F. contributed lively movements, however, but lacked the polish of their opponents in finishing off some praiseworthy efforts.

Tries by W. T. Jones and Douglas Davies, the latter converted by W. E. Jones, put Neath well ahead in the first half, and after the interval W. T. Jones crossed for another pretty try, which W. E. Jones converted. The last score was an unconverted try by D. Lewis.

The match provided good holiday fare, and was a welcome attraction in view of the absence of other holiday amusements. It served to keep one in touch with the rugby code, and was notable for the clean and sportsmanlike manner in which it was contested.

Teams:—

Neath. — Granville Jones; W. T. Jones, Jack Matthews, Douglas Davies, W. H. Clements; W. L. Thomas, W. E. Jones; D. Lewis, Cliff Williams, W. Vickery, Lieut. Irvine, Sergt. Tarrant, H. Thomas, C. Challinor and Hopkin Williams.

R.A.F. — LAC. Ashman; Corporal Williams, AC. Watkins, AC. Griffiths, AC. Swain; F/O Evans, AC. Evans; AC. Hobbs, Cpl. Manfield, AC. Jones, AC. Davies, AC. Shellard, LAC. Healey, LAC. Peyton-Bruel, S/Ldr. White.

Referee: Mr. Ivor David, Neath.

Neath's final wartime games resulted in wins over Cardiff and an RAF XV.

Wartime rugby. The date, venue and opposition are unknown, but among the Neath players taking advantage of this half-time breather are post-war captains Morlais Thomas, Cliff Williams and Tommy James. With his back to the camera wearing a scrum cap is prop Les Anthony, who was capped against Australia after the war. All four youngsters appeared for Neath during their wartime fixtures.

Postscript

The rise of Neath rugby from 1871/72 to the end of the Second World War is a tale of pride, passion, controversy and (all too often) tragedy, but it must be said that researching the history of the Welsh All Blacks has been no hardship for one raised in the Neath tradition.

Hopefully, this publication will have proved of interest both to the modern day rugby fan and to those whose interest lies in historical record. Neath is very much a 'rugby town' and the characters depicted in these pages are therefore part of the town's rich history.

Neath's progress in the post-war rugby world will be charted in a second volume, and the author is currently working on a more comprehensive written history of the first All Blacks.

Undoubtedly there are many more artefacts (photographs, illustrations, season-tickets etc) relating to Neath's rugby past perhaps lying hidden in an attic or at the back of a drawer. The club would be delighted to receive any such ephemera and arrange for display or publication in some future venture.

A far more qualified commentator than the Author once opined, 'In order to understand the present, we must first understand the past.' It is hoped that this publication will have made a small contribution to increasing the reader's comprehension of Neath rugby.